APPROACHES AND CHALLENGES

DIFFERENT PERSPECTIVES FOR BUILDING SHANGHAI FINANCIAL CENTER

路径与挑战

不同视角下的上海国际金融中心建设

贺瑛　张树义　主编

Edited by YING HE, & SHUYI ZHANG

复旦大学出版社
FUDAN UNIVERSITY PRESS

Editors

Ying He	Shanghai Finance University
Shuyi Zhang	Shanghai Finance University

Editorial Boarding

Xiaolu Ying	Shanghai Finance University
Cheng Wanpeng	Shanghai Finance University
Shun-Yu Weng	Takming University of Science and Technology
Wenguo Liu	Shanghai Finance University
Zhiyao Zhang	Queen's University
Dar-Yeh Hwang	National Taiwan University
Yee Ling Chow	The University of Hong Kong
Zheng Fang	Shanghai Finance University

* 编者注：此文中人名拼音据实名编辑，故未作统一。

内容提要

本书是"2013全球金融案例大赛"（2013 Global Finance Case Competition）的报告汇集文集。来自德国、新西兰、匈牙利、坦桑尼亚、津巴布韦、日本、中国大陆、中国台湾和中国香港等地的高校学生，围绕现代金融和科技发展，深入分析全球化背景下的金融中心建设及其金融与科技互动等问题，为上海国际金融中心建设建言献策，本书是各组学生的研究报告合集。

本书可作为高等院校金融学、管理学等专业教学辅助用书，还可作为金融管理、城市规划与发展等政府部门的重要参考书。

Preface for the Global Financial Case Competition Book

Khan Zahid [*]

This book is a compilation of the research-based presentations by the competitors for the Global Financial Case Competition (GFCC) 2013 organized by Shanghai Finance University in Shanghai on August 9-11, 2013. A total of 8 teams from universities around the world were the final participants in the competition, representing countries and regions from Asia, Europe and Africa. They were: the University of Hong Kong, National Taiwan University, Matariki University Network, Takming University of Science and Technology (Taiwan, PRC), Waseda University (Japan), the African Union Team (representing a number of African universities and countries), Budapest College of Communication, Business and Arts, and Shanghai Finance University (SHFU). The competition involved presentations on two cases: (1) Developing an international finance center based on their country/region and its highlights for Shanghai, and (2) Can a hi-tech industry be established in an emerging economy without strong government support?

 The competition was judged by a three-judge panel comprising: (1) Dr. Khan Zahid, Overseas Distinguished Professor of Shanghai

---

[*] Dr. Khan Zahid was the Distinguished Visiting Professor of Shanghai Finance University and Lead Judges for 2013 Global Finance Case Competition held in Shanghai from August 9 to 12, 2013.

 Zahid is an influential Economist in East Asia. He published two treatises on the security market reform and economic history of Saudi Arabia whilst working as a chief economist at Riyad Capital. He initiated an economic research department when working at Riyad Bank, which is one of the excellent institutions in Saudi Arabia afterwards. Zahid often comments on the regional and world economics on the world's major media, Reuters and Bloomberg, for instance. He served for AIG as a chief consultant of CEO about Chinese economics.

Finance University and former Chief Economist of Riyad Capital and Riyad Bank of Saudi Arabia; (2) Prof. Tony McGrew, Dean of the Faculty of Humanities and Social Sciences and Vice President, University of Strathclyde, Glasgow, and (3) Aubrey Chapman, a career banker with over 42 years of professional experience, and a senior Security Expert on anti-financial crimes (AML/CFT).

The first topic was given to the teams in advance and they were required to submit their PowerPoint and research report by August 9th for presentation to the three-judge panel on August 10. The second topic was given to the teams only on the night of August 10th and they had the night to prepare and submit their presentations by early morning of August 11th for presentation on the same day. Each team was judged on three criteria: organization, topic knowledge and presentation. Each team/topic was judged separately by the judges and the team scores for the two topics were totaled at the end. The judges had complete independence and discretion in scoring. The prizes were as follows:

1st Place Winner: Waseda University

2nd Place: University of Hong Kong

3rd Place: Shanghai Finance University

Best Presentation: Waseda University and Matariki University Network

Best Research Team: Waseda, Matariki and SHFU

Best Innovation Team: Budapest College of Communication, Business and Arts

Outstanding Organization: Matariki University Network and SHFU

For Participation and Effort: Takming University of Science and Technology, African Union Team and National Taiwan University.

Several top students were rewarded for Individual Best Presenter, and Individual Best Q&A Performer as well.

The presentations, especially the second case, where they found out about the topic only at the event and had only one night to prepare showed the quality and efforts of all the teams involved. The top three winners — Waseda University, Hong Kong University, and SHFU, the host team — impressed us deeply with the quality of their work and their presentations. They did their homework right and came up with presentations that would have excelled in any other forum. We were particularly impressed by their depth of understanding of the issues involved, their answers to tough questions from the judges and the audience the professionalism of their presentations, and their overall enthusiasm. My own kudos go to them considering that they were mostly sophomores or juniors in college and some of them were not even business finance or economics majors. I was also impressed by the fact that the top teams did not use notes for their presentations or in their Q&A sessions; particular mention goes to the two individuals who won the best presenter and best performer awards.

In the end, however, it is not winning but participating that is most important for these youngsters. They worked hard, gave their best shot and proved their abilities to the utmost. We wish them all good luck in their future studies and careers. They should be proud for participated in this competition. Thanks are also due to Shanghai Finance University, and particularly, Vice President He, for sponsoring the competition and giving the students from around the world to showcase themselves. The organizers — Fang Zheng & Pu Heng, Tan & Wu — deserve exceptional credit for making it a smooth and flawless event. We hope the SHFC will continue the tradition every year and help spread goodwill and professionalism among students around the world, particularly from emerging countries.

Preface

Anthony G. McGrew[*]

It was an honor to be invited by Vice President, Professor He, to participate in the judging panel for the 2013 Global Finance Competition sponsored by Shanghai Finance University. Along with Professor Zahid and Mr Aub Chapman I spent two days on the new campus of the University judging a very lively competition between student teams drawn not just from Chinese universities but from top Asian and European universities too. It was a truly cosmopolitan competition reflecting the globalized nature of the contemporary financial sector. Moreover for me the whole experience was deeply rewarding since the students were most impressive not simply in terms of their individual and collective achievements but just as importantly in their conduct and collective spirit. There was a genuine sense of collaborative learning throughout the two days and an emerging sense of community as the shared experience of the competition bound the students together despite their very different backgrounds, specialisms, abilities, aspirations and cultures. This is an inspirational outcome since it speaks to an optimistic and practical vision of universities as places

---

[*] Professor Anthony G. McGrew is the Dean of the Faculty of Humanities and Social Sciences, and Vice President of University of Strathclyde, Glasgow. His research Interests focus on Economic Globalization, Global Governance, China and Global Institutions. He was a visiting professor or fellow at many universities, such as Ritsumeikan University (Kyoto), Australian National University, LSE, Chuo University (Tokyo), Nanjing University of Finance and Economics, and institutions, Shanghai Academy of Social Sciences, for instance. He has published many academic papers on top journals, and authored many books on Globalization, Politics, and Economics. His current Projects and Publications in Progress are Economic Globalization after the Financial Crisis, and the "Rise" of China and Global Governance.

not just for academic learning, but also as building blocks of a global community in an increasingly interconnected world. An intangible prize, which all who competed over those two days will benefit directly from as they seek to build their careers in the globalized world of finance.

As to the substantive competition itself, this was superbly organized under the auspices of Professor He and Professor Shuyi Zhang. For the competitors, it was a very demanding two days in which a pre-prepared presentation on a topic was given by each team delivered in English and subject to live questioning by the judging panel. There were some absolutely outstanding presentations and dialogues with the judges, both by individual students and teams. The second day consisted of presentations on a topic which teams were given at the close of the first day of the competition. This was a very rigorous test of each team's ability to work collaboratively and effectively researching, organizing, and delivering a presentation on a topic upon which they had no prior warning or knowledge. It proved a really tough but valuable challenge for all the teams, all of which did exceptionally well in delivering very professional presentations with little more than twelve hours notice. Most worked overnight and this built a strong sense of camaraderie and collective purpose within and across teams, a formative experience for all concerned. Given these tough conditions the overall standard of presentations was extremely high. Quite a few were inspiring and simply first class. This was reflected in the judges comments and the awarding of many generous prizes both for teams and individual students.

In addition to the actual competition I joined the participants on several arranged activities including a visit to the ICBC Museum in Pudong. This was extremely informative. It was also facilitated by the many senior alumni of the University given SFU's pivotal position, long tradition, and reputation in supplying Shanghai's banking and financial sector with well qualified graduates and postgraduates.

The 2013 SFU Global Finance Competition was a very impressive event. In the annual calendar of such competitions it stands out for its innovation, cosmopolitanism, and outstanding hospitality in one of the world's emerging global financial centers. For students of finance and banking it offers a wonderful cosmopolitan learning experience. It has been a privilege and a great pleasure judging the 2013 competition.

Preface

William A. Chapman[*]

At the outset, I must congratulate Professor He Ying, Vice President of the Shanghai Finance University and Professor Shuyi Zhang, Vice Dean of the School of Innovation and Entrepreneurship at the Shanghai Finance University together with the organizing committee for creating and delivering such an innovative competition involving undergraduate teams from 8 universities from a number of diverse countries/regions and cultural backgrounds.

In joining with Professor Anthony McGrew from Strathclyde

---

[*] Prior to his retirement from Westpac Banking Corporation in September 2003, William Aub Chapman was a career banker with over 42 years of professional experience. He has extensive experience in a range of areas including Audit, Major IT projects, Fraud Control, AML/CFT and Sanctions, Cash and ATM Services, Physical Security and Business Continuity Planning.

Aub has been involved with fraud and anti-money laundering controls since 1991 and has appeared as a technical expert before several Australian parliamentary committees including one which examined the operational effectiveness of Australia's AML legislation. Aub has appeared before the Victorian Parliamentary Enquiry into Electronic Commerce and has presented papers at and chaired the Australian Fraud Summit on several occasions and has co-authored papers for the Australian Institute of Criminology.

Since his retirement from Westpac, Aub has focused on providing consulting services in relation to AML/CFT/Sanctions and controls against other Financial Crimes. He has made numerous presentations and facilitated a number of conferences on controls against money laundering both within Australia and overseas. He has also been involved in international AML/CFT consulting assignments on behalf the United Nations, the Asian Development Bank, the Eurasian Group on Combating Money Laundering and the Financial Services Volunteer Corp.

Aub's experience and expertise was recognized in 2009 when he received the AML Professional of the Year Award at the Association of Anti-Money Laundering Specialists International Conference held in the United States.

University and Professor Khan Zahid of the Shanghai Finance University as the panel of judges, I have been privileged to witness the drive and enthusiasm that the competitors displayed in presenting their findings for a pre-announced assignment on the first day and then, under considerable time pressure and with limited research facilities being available, working overnight through a second assignment which was announced at the close of day one, to present their findings for this second case on day two of the competition. This drive and enthusiasm was even more surprising considering that a number of students participating do not have finance as their primary field of study. The fact that the competition required the teams to produce their case papers and present their findings in English added to the challenge for a number of the competitors.

While the 8 teams were competing for valuable cash prizes, I feel that each team also gained valuable experience by participating in this competition and in front of a panel of judges from a variety of backgrounds and disciplines.

It was no surprise to see that certain teams and certain participants within the teams displayed a greater level of confidence and knowledge of the subject matter. What I did find pleasing was the improvement evident on day two compared with the day one performances by a number of the teams and this is an encouraging indicator of the tertiary-level discipline shown by these young students.

I found the underlying concept for the 2013 Global Finance Case Competition to be sound from a competitive perspective. In my opinion, the framework within which the judging panel assigned scores for each team over the two days also provided an appropriate level of rigor to the process and the resulting aggregate scores.

I commend the decision to publish the teams' reports of the two case studies. This will not only prove a valuable resource for other students, but it will also provide the competition participants with an opportunity to analyse the approach taken and the findings presented by the other teams. I consider this to be an added learning opportunity that should enhance each competitor's knowledge regarding International Finance Centers and factors that influence the success or otherwise of such centers and their impact on a country's economic strength.

In conclusion, I would encourage Shanghai Finance University to continue with and expand this excellent initiative as a means of promoting cooperation among like-minded universities throughout the world and advancing financial knowledge at the undergraduate level.

CONTENTS

Chapter 1   The Development of Tokyo International Financial Center and Its Enlightenment for Shanghai
Li Shenru, Hidemi Kurita, Taewoong Kim, Nicole Lee
Waseda University Team

1	Introduction	1
2	The Development of Tokyo as a Financial Center	4
3	Experience and Lessons Learned from Tokyo Experiences: Positioned to Serve the Real Economy	10
4	Tokyo's Enlightenment for Shanghai	14
	References	16

Chapter 2   Building the Global Financial Centre — The Path and Evidence from Hong Kong
Jinhao Chen, Harry Au, Karry Kong, Jordan Shin
The University of Hong Kong Team

1	Introduction	18
2	Methodology	21
3	Quality of Financial Product & Product Diversity	21
4	Strengthening Supervision by Regulations	28
5	Development of Modern Business and Communications	

	Infrastructure	31
6	Building and Education of Human Capital and Financial Talents	35
7	Limitations	37
8	Conclusions	38
	References	40
	Appendices	41

Chapter 3 Building the International Financial Center: Path and Highlights for Shanghai
Rujia Wang, Xina Liu, Xiaokai Jin, Yashu Li
Shanghai Finance University Team

1	Financial History of Shanghai	45
2	Shanghai's Relative Advantages and Disadvantages Compared with Other IFCs	49
3	Some Existing Prominent Problems	55
4	Future Orientation of Shanghai IFC	61
5	Conclusions	65
	References	66

Chapter 4 Shanghai International Financial Center
Hsin-Jen Wen, Hsiao-Ting Huang, Bei-Yu Gao, Tzu-Han Kao
Takming University of Science and Technology Team

1	The Purpose of Project	68

2	The Advantages of the Financial Center	70
3	The Establishment of Shanghai International Financial Center	71
4	Summary	74
	References	74

Chapter 5 Shanghai Finance Center and Africa's Experiences
Doreen Kifumani, Saunath Tayah, Jonathan Muromba
African Union Team

1	What Is a Financial Center?	76
2	Why Do We Study Financial Centers?	77
3	What Are the Global Financial Centers Today?	80
4	What Are the Key Lessons for Shanghai from All These Comparisons?	85
5	Shanghai Financial Center and Hong Kong Financial Center	91
6	Conclusions	95
	References	96

Chapter 6 Shanghai Budapest Business Bridge
Roland Kapros, Agenlla Serafin
Budapest College of Communication, Business and Arts Team

1	What Is a Global Financial Center?	98
2	Why Do Financial Centers Exist in Our Electronic Age?	99
3	What Are the Benefits of Being Such a Center?	100
4	General Attribute of Hungary	100

5	Why Budapest Could Be the Financial Center of East-Central Europe?	100
6	Plan: Budapest Gate	105
7	Shanghai-Budapest Business Bridge	106
8	Conclusion	110
	References	111

Chapter 7 Turning Taipei into an International Financial Center
Shou-Han Liu, En-Ti Hwang, Tien-Yung Chou, Shao-Yi Peng
National Taiwan University Team

1	What Is an International Financial Center?	112
2	Taiwan	113
3	Why Can We Turn Taipei into an International Financial Center?	113

Chapter 8 The Development and Future of Shanghai as an International Financial Center
LING Quincy, OSWALD Kolja, TURNBULL Mahoney
Matariki University Network Team

1	Introduction	118
2	Methodologies	120
3	Frankfurt as a Case Study	122
4	Shanghai as an IFC	125
5	Conclusions	139
	References	140

Chapter 1

The Development of Tokyo International Financial Center and Its Enlightenment for Shanghai

Li Shenru,[1] Hidemi Kurita[2], Taewoong Kim,[3] Nicole Lee[4]
Waseda University Team

Introduction

The Tokyo international financial center is an important reference for Shanghai. The development of Tokyo financial center has several similarities with Shanghai. For example, financial development is closely related to internationalization of local currency; their governments largely pushed development; both have experience of rapid economic growth. This paper will explain the development of Tokyo as an international financial center, and discuss the experience and lessons learned from Tokyo by way of examples. Section 1 will focus on the current position of Tokyo, while Sections 2-4 will relatively give a description of the development of Tokyo as an

---

[1] Shenru Li is an undergraduate in School of Political Science and Economics at Waseda University, Japan.
[2] Hidemi Kurita is an undergraduate in School of International Liberal Studies at Waseda University, Japan.
[3] Taewoong Kim is an undergraduate in School of International Liberal Studies at Waseda University, Japan.
[4] Nicole Lee is an undergraduate in School of International Liberal Studies at Waseda University, Japan.

international financial center, the experience and lessons learned from Tokyo, and Tokyo's enlightenment for Shanghai.

1 Importance of Tokyo as an International Financial Center

Generally speaking, Tokyo is a recognized international financial center. Global Financial Center Index (GFCI), which is recognized as an indicator system for international financial centers, gives Tokyo a high rating as well. Table 1-1 shows the rating and ranking of Tokyo by GFCI from GFCI1 (2007) to GFCI13 (2013). Except GFCI5 (2009.3), Tokyo secured its ranking in the Top 10, which indicates that Tokyo has a stable performance in global financial activities.

Table 1-1 Ranking and Rating of Tokyo from GFCI1 to GFCI13

	Ranking	Rating
GFCI1(March 2007)	9	632
GFCI2(September 2007)	10	625
GFCI3(March 2008)	9	628
GFCI4(Sepetember 2008)	7	642
GFCI5(March 2009)	15	611
GFCI6(Sepetember 2009)	7	674
GFCI7(March 2010)	5	692
GFCI8(September 2010)	5	697
GFCI9(March 2011)	5	694
GFCI10(September 2011)	6	695
GFCI11(March 2012)	5	693
GFCI12(September 2012)	7	684
GFCI13(March 2013)	6	718

Source: QFC, the Global Financial Centers Index 2013

The status of Tokyo international financial center is stable and sustainable. According to GFCI 2013 assessment, Tokyo ranked top-10 in all the five areas of competitiveness. "Five areas of competitiveness" are five groups of instrumental factors, and these groups are respectively: people, business environment, market access, infrastructure, and general competitiveness. Table 1-2 shows the detailed ranking of Tokyo in these areas. Just like mentioned before, Tokyo ranked 6th in people, 8th in business environment, 8th in market access, 7th in infrastructure, and 7th in general competitiveness. This fact indicates that, the change range of Tokyo's performance is relatively narrow, because even one of these areas is crippled, other areas will still perform well and help to promote the crippled area. A financial center can not necessarily rank highly in all the ranges; for example, Seoul ranked 9th and 10th relatively in infrastructure and general competitiveness, but its rating in people, the business environment and market access are out of top 10. Compared to Seoul, Tokyo is sustainable in terms of development.

Table 1-2　Five Areas of Competitiveness Top 10

Rank	People	Business environment	Market access	Infrastructure	General competitiveness
1	London(-)	London(-)	London(-)	London(-)	London(-)
2	New York (-)	New York (-)	New York (-)	New York(-)	New York(-)
3	Hong Kong (-)	Hong Kong (-)	Hong Kong (-)	Hong Kong (-)	Hong Kong (-)
4	Singapore (-)	Singapore (-)	Singapore (-)	Singapore(-)	Singapore(-)
5	Zurich(-)	Zurich(-)	Zurich(-)	Zurich(-)	Zurich(-)
6	Tokyo(-)	Geneva(-)	Geneva(-)	Boston(+6)	Boston(+6)
7	Boston(+4)	Boston(+4)	Boston(+2)	Tokyo(+2)	Tokyo(-)
8	Geneva(+2)	Tokyo(-)	Tokyo(-1)	Geneva(-1)	Geneva(-)
9	Frankfurt (+2)	Frankfurt (-)	Frankfurt (+1)	Seoul(-3)	Frankfurt (+1)

continued

Rank	People	Business environment	Market access	Infrastructure	General competitiveness
10	Toronto(-1)	Chicago(-1)	Chicago(-3)	Frankfurt(-1)	Seoul(-4)

Source: QFC, the Global Financial Centers Index 2013

Tokyo's performance in industrial sectors verified its sustainability as well. Table 1-3 shows Tokyo's ranking in industrial sectors. Tokyo ranked higher in all the five industries, which made its development sustainable.

Table 1-3 Tokyo's ranking in Industrial Sectors

Industry	Rank
Investment Management	5(-)
Banking	6(-)
Government & regulatory	7(-)
Insurance	8(-2)
Professional services	9(+5)

Source: QFC, the Global Financial Centers Index 2013

Other factors also contribute to Tokyo's performance. For example, Tokyo's good reputation in the financial market (which ranked 2nd according to GFCI 2013 report) and its stability (labeled "dynamic" according to GFCI 2013).

All these observations indicate that, Tokyo is a dynamic financial center; it fully deserves the name of regional financial center with stability and reputation. We have a bright outlook on Tokyo's future performance.

2   The Development of Tokyo as Financial Center

2.1   Background

The background of financial internationalization is the internationalization of the real economy. From 1970s, Japan's export volume ascended rapidly. In 1970 Japan's total export was 7,926 billion yen, which occupied 10.8% of GDP; in 1980 total export reached 32,887 billion yen, which was 13.7% of GDP, and in 1985 total export and its proportion of GDP were respectively 46,307 billion yen and 14.5%. The needs and activities of export gave rise to finance liberalization.

Increasing net foreign asset is another aspect of Japan's financial liberalization. Because of the large amount of surplus in the current account, the demand for foreign asset expanded rapidly. Japan's net foreign asset increased from 10.9 billion dollars in 1981, to 129.8 billion dollars in 1985. Even after the burst of bubble, Japan's net foreign asset kept expanding, and the expansion of net foreign asset was one of the reasons of finance internationalization.

2.2 The process of financial internationalization

The process of Japan's financial internationalization includes: the liberalization of trade finance, cross-border financial transaction, and local financial market; the internationalization of yen and local financial institutions. Table 2-1 shows the detailed process of Japan's financial internationalization.

Table 2-1 Detailed Process of Japan's Financial Internationalization

1980.12	Foreign Exchange Law revised
1983.6	Liberalization of short-term Euro-Japanese Credit for non-residents
1984.5	Publication of Yen/Dollar committee's Report
1984.6	Free convertibility of yen
1985.4	Liberalization of yen long-term Euro-Japanese Credit for non-residents
1985.6	Set up BA market quote in yen
1986.12	Set up Tokyo offshore market
1989.7	Liberalization of long-term Euro-Japanese Credit for residents

Among these incidents, the revise of Foreign Exchange Law was a crucial one. Before 1980, for the sake of international payment balance, Japan strictly implemented foreign exchange management. Because of the revision of the foreign exchange law, the capital movement was principally liberalized. The revision made the liberalization of Euro-Japanese Credit possible, and facilitated the free convertibility of yen.

The establishment of a Yen/Dollar Committee heavily contributed to the internationalization of the yen as well. In the report published in May 1984, three conclusions were reached: first, to liberalize Japan's financial and capital market, including liberalization of exchange rates, and free convertibility of yen; second, to improve the business environment of Japan's financial and capital market, including the foreign security companies' ownership of membership of the Tokyo Stock Exchange, and foreign banks' penetration to trust services; and the third, to expand the yen's European market.

With the help of Yen/Dollar committee, Japan accelerated its pace of financial internationalization. The interest rate was liberalized; the financial regulation was loosened; International Securities Trading expanded. It is worth mentioning that along with financial internationalization, the trading volume of foreign stocks and bonds by Japanese residents increased rapidly. Foreign bonds bought by Japanese residents grew from 73 trillion yen in 1985 to 278 trillion yen; the financing of overseas funds by Japanese enterprises increased from 8 billion yen in 1985 to 11 trillion yen in 1989; the same thing happened to Samurai bonds and Euro-yen bonds, whose issued amount boomed from 373 billion yen in 1980, to 5.7 trillion in 1990.

Financial liberalization brought the opportunity of development to Tokyo. In 1980s, rather than national finance center, Tokyo developed into an international financial center. Tokyo became an advanced financial market in terms of numbers of practitioners and transaction scale. Figure 2–1 shows the asset, saving and loan volume of Japanese banking industry from 1980 to 2004, and it indicates that these variations increased stably until 1990s.

Figure 2-1   The Development of Banking Industry (entity: trillion yen)

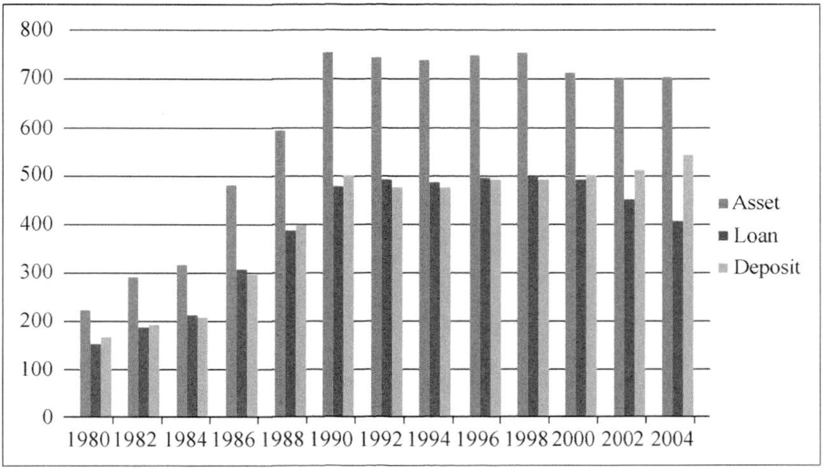

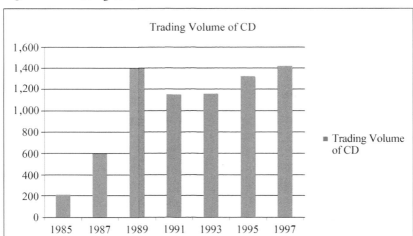

Source: Statistics Bureau of Japan

Figure 2-2   Trading Volume of CD

Source: Bank of Japan

Figure 2-3   Nikkei 225, 1980-2006

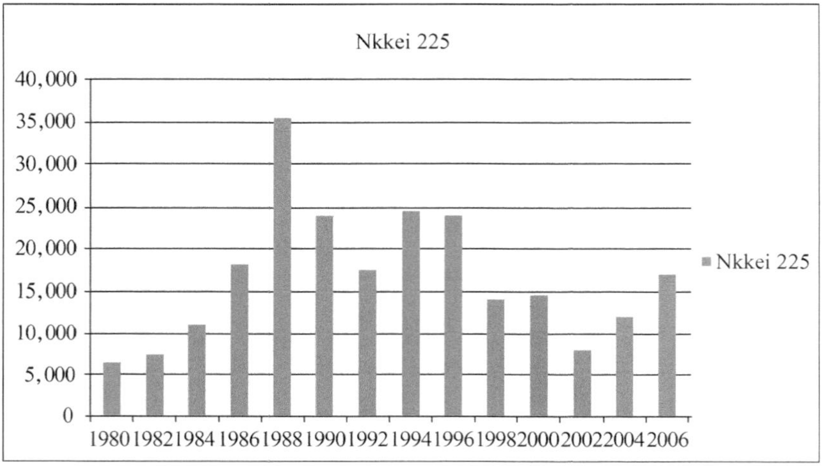

[Bar chart titled "Nkkei 225" showing Nkkei 225 values from 1980 to 2006, with values ranging from about 6,000 in 1980, rising to a peak of about 35,000 around 1988, then declining with fluctuations to about 17,000 by 2006.]

Source: Tokyo Stock Exchange

Other financial markets in Tokyo also benefited from financial liberalization. Figure 2-2 and Figure 2-3 respectively show the boom of certificate deposit and stock exchange market. The boom of these two markets indicates that, financial liberalization brought Tokyo a great chance to evolve from a national financial center to an international financial center, and to ascend to one of the most important financial centers in the world in 1980s.

2.3   The burst of bubble and the fall of Tokyo

After the bubble burst, the Japanese economy stagnated for more than 10 years. Japanese economy reached its lowest point in October 1993, and recovered in March 1997. Unfortunately, because of the tax policy and financial reform, the Japanese economy went down again. In financial markets, the regression influenced the whole industry.

First, the efficiency of investment largely decreased. During the bubble economy period, most of the investment did not help to promote total productivity. As a result, after the burst of bubble, investment levels declined sharply, and it was revealed that social saving was not invested in profitable projects. Therefore, the bubble burst led to the insufficient demand, and it also resulted in economic stagnation due to inefficient reallocation of resources.

Second, the banking industry was heavily shocked because of the depreciation of assets. The depreciation of assets left banks in insolvency crisis. The equity capital of banks was corroded, which led to risk aversion in banks' activity in 1990s. More specifically, enterprises were reluctant to invest or expand production, and financial institutions suffered a loan drought. Affected by risk aversion of the whole society, deposits were not likely to flow to high risk high reward fields. It was the flow of deposits that made the economy stagnate for a long period of time.

With the burst of bubble, non-performing loans (NPL) also became a problem for the banking industry. Given that NPL accumulated in the banking system, banks could hardly serve as the intermediate of an accommodation line.

2.4 Revival of Tokyo as an international financial center

In order to solve the "hollowing out" problem, Prime Minister Hashimoto issued the "Financial Big Bang" reform plan. The plan was mainly about the deregulation of the financial service industry and the protection of investors and market justice. A new Foreign Exchange law was issued in 1998, and its context included two aspects: one was the total liberalization of equity trading; the other was the abolishment of the license system of foreign exchange banks. Besides the revised law, the content of reform included: promotion of the management of the NPL and profitability of the bank sector, the introduction of the horizontal rule system, and other policies. However, the plan did not achieve its expected aim; in 2007, Tokyo still ranked the 10th on the GFCI indicator system. Given the situation, Japan issued new financial exchange laws in 2007, promoting the revival plan of Tokyo international financial center.

3 Experience and Lessons Learned from Tokyo Experiences: Positioned to Serve Real Economy

Tokyo financial market is positioned to serve real economy. The advanced banking industry, stock market and finance derivative market mainly offered services to the real economy industries rather than financial industries. With the help of financial institutions, Japanese enterprises got enough resources to expand production and improve technological innovation.

Although it is hard to deny that the burst of bubble is responsible for Japanese economic stagnation in 1990s, the incomplete structural

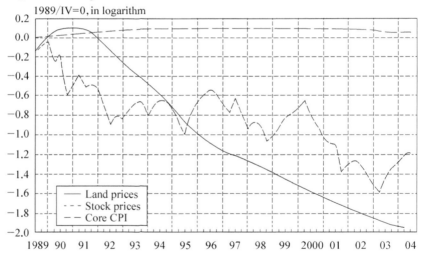

Figure 3-1 Depreciation of Asset Price

Note: CPI excluding fresh food is seasonally adjusted by X-12-ARIMA with options of (0 1 2)(0 1 1) ARIMA model and level shifts in April 1989 and April 1997, when the consumption tax was respectively introduced and subsequently hiked.

Sources: Bank of Japan, "Financial and Economic Statistics Monthly"; Ministry of Public Management, Home Affairs, Posts and Telecommunications, "Consumer Price Index"; Japan Real Estate Institute, "Urban Land Price Index."

adjustment still plays a crucial role in the fall of Tokyo as an international financial center.

In 1990s Japanese financial market experienced the depreciation of asset price. Figure 3-1 shows the detailed information of the depreciation. At the same time, growth tended to go downward (Figure 3-2). Views were divided on these issues; two views became the mainstream, one of which claimed that insufficiency in aggregate demand is the main reason of economic stagnation, while the other one stated that, it was structural problems that led to the stagnation. The history proved that the latter explanation was the correct one.

Non-performing loans, globalization and demographic changes contributed to the changes in economic structure. Figure 3-3 shows the NPL-nominal GDP ratio in 1990s. The increasing NPL were mainly caused by lending to inefficient firms (also called "zombie firms"), which were obstacles to efficient resource reallocation. Offering loans to the unproductive industries is not likely to help the structural shift from unproductive industry to productive industry. Figure 3-4 shows

Figure 3-2　Output Growth Rate

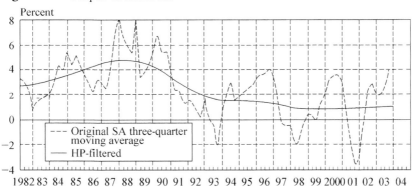

Note: Real GDP on a 93SNA basis. The HP-filtered series is computed for the period from 1980/I to 2002/III by using the smoothing parameter $\lambda = 1,600$.

Sources: Bank of Japan, "Financial and Economic Statistics Monthly"; Cabinet Office, "National Accounts."

Figure 3-3 NPL-nominal GDP Ratio

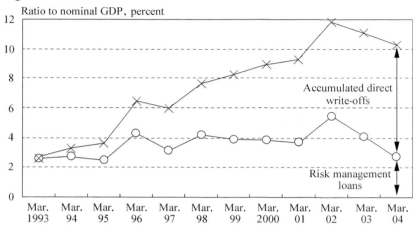

Notes: 1. Figures are summations of data for city banks, long-term credit banks, and trust banks. (Data for all banks and all deposit-taking institutions are not available before March 1996.)
2. Risk management loans are summations of loans to borrowers in legal bankruptcy, past-due loans in arrears for six months or more, and loans in arrears by three months or more and less than six months.

Source: Financial Services Agency (http://www.fsa.go.jp); Cabinet Office, "National Accounts."

the change in ROE and ROA of different industries in 1990s Japan, and these figures indicate the declining profitability in all the industries. These observations suggest that, the resource reallocation in financial markets did not proceed smoothly.

Globalization impacted the competitiveness of Japanese industries as well. For example, the rise of China in 1990s heavily influenced employment in Japan. The reallocation of employment created and destroyed jobs, forced Japan to shift its industrial structure in response to the rise of other economies. Besides these factors, demographic change also played a significant role in structure change. Figure 3-2 shows the demographic trend of Japan in 1990s, and the figure indicates the decline of fertility rate and ascent of the proportion of

Figure 3-4 ROE and ROA

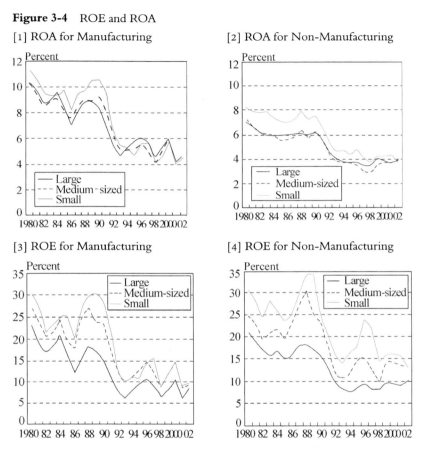

Source: Ministry of Finance, "Financial Statements Statistics of Corporations by Industry, Quarterly"

aging people. The aging trend added a burden to the social security system, increasing the saving rate of household, and caused difficulties in promoting productivity.

Under such circumstances, the Japanese government issued a series of monetary and fiscal policies — and all these policies were criticized because they were more aggressive and more expansionary. When the potential growth rate is experiencing a decline, the effectiveness of fiscal and monetary policies will differ from that in normal conditions. In 1990s, the Japanese government injected more than 2 percent of GDP (10 trillion yen) to the banks sector, but the result, as mentioned before, turned out to be disappointing. The reason is that the injection of capital did not stop banks from offering loans to zombie firms; as a result, the process of structural change was impeded. To prevent this from happening, the Japanese government could intervene more in the capital market; however, the government was reluctant to decide whether to intervene more in the market and the hesitation worsened the situation.

Some critics considered fiscal expenditure by Japanese government to be a sufficiently expansionary, because of the increasing government deficit. It is true that from 1990s the government deficit increased at a surprising speed, however, it is largely related to the unsustainable pension system, and the influence of demographic change. Given the change of fiscal expenditure and social security system expenditure were synchronized, it can be inferred that the increasing government expenditure partly went to the pension system, and the capital used for stimulus policies, however, did not change a lot. That is, fiscal policies could be more aggressive.

As a conclusion of this section, the insufficient structure reform and government interventions contributed to the financial sector's failure in serving real economy efficiently, and finally resulted in the continuing regression of economy. Besides the factors listed above, other factors such as rigidified financial regulation, insufficient English-speaking practitioners, and Japanese traditional attitude to finance industry (considering finance as a dirty industry) were lessons learned from Tokyo as well.

4   Tokyo's Enlightenment for Shanghai

Tokyo is an important reference for Shanghai in terms of an international financial center. The development of the Tokyo financial center has three features: 1) the development is closely related to the internationalization of yen; 2) the development is related to the rapid development of the domestic economy; 3) the government has largely pushed development. These features also appeared in the development process of Shanghai. Similar to Tokyo, Shanghai is in a rapid development period; the internationalization of the Renminbi is in process, and the central government has issued a series of supportive policies to promote the development of the international financial center.

Tokyo's enlightenment of Shanghai includes:

1) Shanghai international financial center should be positioned to serve the real economy. It should serve the trade financing and production financing; its positioning should be related to capital operation, offering advanced service such as M&A, IPO, investment and financing arrangements. The Shanghai financial center should be the center of financial and economic transaction as well as a relocation center of international and domestic financial reform.

2) Shanghai international financial center should be developed from a national financial center, to a regional center, and finally become an international financial center.

Shanghai may be developed as a "double hinterland". "Double hinterland" means that, Shanghai should simultaneously become an economic hinterland and information hinterland. Shanghai already has an economic hinterland now, but it is not enough. The development of financial center relies on information. To trading, an industry chain is more important than a trading platform; the head offices of financial institutions themselves are industry chains. Therefore, transactions are more likely to gather in the city where head offices are located. The head offices of institutions are the largest information source. However, in China, most of the financial institutions set up their head offices in Beijing. Since the relocation of head offices is costly, an acceptable solution is to set up a Shanghai head office.

Shanghai international financial center needs government support. The development of the financial center needs joint effort of central government, local authorities and financial market. Shanghai has the ability to integrate these efforts, and become an international financial center.

References

Kazuo U. (2009). *The Structure of Japan's Financial Regulation and Supervision and the Role Played by the Bank of Japan, After the Fall: Re-evaluating Supervisory, Regulatory, and Monetary Policy*, Cape Cod, October 21-23.

Qatar Financial Center. (2013). *The Global Financial Center Index 2013*.

Kunio O., and Shigenori S. (2004). Asset Price Fluctuations, Structural Adjustments, and Sustained Economic Growth: Lessons from Japan's Experience since the Late 1980s, *Monetary and Economic Studies* (Special Edition), December.

Sayuri S. (2007). *Promoting Tokyo as an International Financial Center*. Available at http://www.cfci.org.cn/Images/UploadFile/D_20101105/20101105102744.pdf.

Kindleberger, C. P., and C. Poor. (1973). *The Formation of Financial Centers: A study in Comparative Economic Study*. Available at http://hdl.handle.net/1721.1/63624.

Chandrasekhar, C. P. (2003). Finance and the Real Economy: The Global Conjuncture, *Canadian Journal of Development Studies*, 24(2), 215-227.

Chapter 2

Building the Global Financial Center — the Path and Evidence from Hong Kong

Jinhao Chen [1], Harry Au [2], Karry Kong [3], Jordan Shin [4]
The University of Hong Kong Team
Coach: Yee Ling Chow[*]

With the emergence of China as a global economic powerhouse, its financial capital Shanghai has also become a city of strategic importance. In its most recent 12th 5 Year Plan of Financial Development and Reformation, the Chinese government aims to develop Shanghai into an international financial center by 2020.

With reference to the 5 Year Plan, the future development of Shanghai can be focused on 4 areas, namely improving the current financial growth model, strengthening of financial regulation and supervision, developing proper infrastructure, and lastly, cultivating and attracting talents. By mainly comparing it with 2 successful models

---

[1] Jinhao Chen is an undergraduate majoring in Wealth Management at the University of Hong Kong.
[2] Harry Au is an undergraduate majoring in Public Administration, Global Studies and Sociology at the University of Hong Kong.
[3] Karry Kong is an undergraduate majoring in Accounting and Finance at the University of Hong Kong.
[4] Jordan Shih is an undergraduate majoring in Economics and Finance at the University of Hong Kong.
[*] Yee Ling Chow (Elaine) is a staff who is in charge of student affairs in the University of Hong Kong.

of Asian financial center, Hong Kong and Singapore, it can be seen that while Shanghai is well developed in many aspects, it is still relatively weak or lacking certain elements in these 4 areas.

Shanghai's financial growth model requires revamping it needs to build up the size and variety of its insurance market. It should also expand its bond market to shake off the over-reliance on overseas and bank financing, and develop a greater secondary market. Its equity market also requires greater foreign capital input and the swift introduction of a more diverse group of financial products. It also needs to alter its current regulation and supervision policy so as not to inhibit growth, but at the same time enforce the rule of law and instill confidence in investors. Regulations should be changed from rules based to principles based to instill a positive mentality from the senior management level. As for infrastructure, further improvements can be made to its intra and intercity transport system, as well as its telecommunication network. Lastly, immigration policies can be loosened so as to increase the inflow of human capital.

However, with such a huge population base and rapidly growing economy, it may be unrealistic to monitor all financial transactions under one single authority. The huge information cost of regulation and supervision may also impede the progress of reforms. Hence such policies for change should be tailor-made for Shanghai's unique economic and demographic environment to ensure Shanghai's development as an international financial center.

1 Introduction

Inspired by the success of some international financial centers worldwide, we could easily compare some common features and characteristics of these cities and countries which could be used for reference for some potential and developing financial hubs — especially Shanghai. The examples could be New York, London, Hong Kong and Singapore. In this report, we would focus on the main aims regarding Shanghai's "12th 5 Year Plan of Financial Development and

Reformation" and provide some practical recommendations based on references from these developed financial cities.

A good financial hub is often recognized by its technological advances and low transport and communications costs where businessmen and entrepreneurs are willing to put their money in investment and starting up their businesses. A report from the Security Industry Association in New York stated out that there would be some factors which a good international financial center would possess. The stronger these elements they have, the greater chances they would attract world-class talents and investments.

First, the financial center has to be in a stable and open political and economic regime. Second, the legal system, regulations and tax regimes should be fair and transparent. Third, there should be a skilled labor force and strong talent support. Fourth, the cost of doing and starting a business is always low and affordable. Fifth, the implementation of international standards and practices such as IOSCO should be strictly followed. Lastly, the physical infrastructure should be of high quality and quantity.

1.1   The importance of Asian cities in global finance

Asia is seen as an important region for the OECD in terms of its members and partners. The OECD is a Paris-based policy institution and is regarded as Euro-centric. Take Japan as an example, it became a member three years after the foundation of OECD. Soon China, Indonesia and India were adopted to be its key partners in Asia (Republic, October 2008). Besides, Asia has shown good handling of the global financial crisis since it provides a stabilizing force when the economic situations in the western world become problematic.

1.2   The importance of China in global finance and economics

China underwent probably the most striking economic changes back to the last 20 years. The role China played in global finance has become more and more apparent. These include the rise of Chinese corporations and their significance around the world; the growth of China's region exchange reserve; the increase of multi-national brands and integrated businesses; the potential of consumer demand and habits and the penetration of internet and mobile phone uses (Cainey, 2010). The size and capabilities of the financial institutions, the banks and the capital markets have ever increased these last few years.

1.3 Shanghai and the 12th 5 Year Plan of Financial Development and Reformation

In 2010, the Chinese government's State Council announced a clear goal for Shanghai to become a mature international financial center by 2020. The first aim is to make it a financial hub in accordance with China's economic strength. Second, Shanghai's goal has to be raising the international status of Reminbi.

Based on the framework of 12th 5 Year Plan of Financial Development and Reformation, our group has concluded some factors essential for Shanghai's success, and also the methods which could be taken as important for building up Shanghai as an international financial center.

The first point to be noted is that there should be change from the current financial growth model. That is, the financial products developed and derived from the markets should be both of good quality and diversified quantity, especially in the segment of bond holdings and equity.

The second is to strengthen supervision by regulation. This should be completed with sound financial supervision by the authorities, together with a strong back-up risk management system.

The third point is the development of the business infrastructure and human resources infrastructure. These two elements could strongly support the city financial development not only physically but also mentally.

The last point to make is the building and education of human capital and financial talents. With stricter and more flexible labor laws enforced, we believe that talent could show its strength and provide wisdom for Shanghai to become an international financial city.

2 Methodology

In order to provide suggestions for the future financial development of Shanghai, this report will mainly focus on 4 crucial reformations in "12th 5 Year Plan of Chinese Financial Development and Reformation". Since Hong Kong and Singapore have some similarities (i.e. consist of Chinese people) with Shanghai, this research will compare Shanghai with the other two cities: take the two cities as models and extract suitable features from their financial development, to shape the financial development of Shanghai.

3 Quality of Financial Product & Product Diversity

3.1 Goals to be achieved

There is no denying about Asia's recent financial success. Since the last Asian financial crisis, Asian economies, especially financial centers like Hong Kong and Singapore, have emerged at the forefront of global production and financial activity. However, Asia still lags behind western economies like the US and the UK in terms of market capitalization and the diversity of financial products.

Insurance

Insurance premiums have already taken over other products such as bonds and equities to become the greatest source of income for the financial industry. With the current trend of institutional and private investors becoming ever more reliant on insurance products, it is important for Shanghai to develop a mature insurance market with a comprehensive regulatory framework.

Bond

The crisis of the late 1990s had already called for mature and developed regional bond markets in Asia. However, most economies were slow to react and Asia's debt capital markets suffered once again during the 2008 financial crisis, due to little primary market issuance and widening secondary performance. As Shanghai aims to become a global financial center, one of its first goals will, therefore, be to create a debt market of substantial breadth and depth.

Equities and other products

The best measure for a city's financial development is perhaps the extent of equity financing and the degree of market capitalization. Hence Shanghai should focus on attracting a greater amount of capital to its equities market. In addition, derivatives such as options and futures are key components of a developed equity market as they add to the breadth of the capital market. Being important credit risk relief tools, the derivative markets in Shanghai should be formulated and stabilized gradually in the coming years just like other financial cities.

3.2 Insurance

Current situation in Shanghai

Shanghai has its own insurance regulations and the Shanghai Insurance Association regulates the insurance bodies. However, according to the news in July 2013, Shanghai's insurance industry and transactions were trapped in a weak stage. This could be partly accounted for by the fact of weak short-term insurance demand in the markets, tighter mobility and liquidity of products and low investment return. Compared with Hong Kong and Japan, the insurance expansion of Shanghai was in a slow and decreasing pace which is pessimistic in the current markets.

Reflections from other international financial cities

The Hong Kong insurance market not only contains the element of general insurance, but also long-term insurance. General insurance is easily defined as accident and health, aircraft, goods in transit, property damage, general damage, general liability, motor vehicle and employees' compensation. However, the Hong Kong insurance market focuses more on long-term insurance including non-linked and linked individual life, group life, and retirement schemes. Recently, MPF-Mandatory Provident Fund is also one of the main focus in the financial sales industry. According to a paper in HKTDC Research in

2012, there was a total income of around 29.1 billion USD made by the insurance markets in 2011 in Hong Kong, with 85% made from the long-term insurance businesses. There are more than 9291 registered insurance-related organizations in 2012. The industry is regulated by the Office of Commissioner of Insurance which administers the Insurance Companies Ordinance.

Similarly, the Singapore insurance industry comprises the general insurance and life insurance. Until 2008, the total insurance premium made by the Singapore insurance market was up to 16.5 billion USD. The success on its markets lies on the fact that MAS takes a pro-active approach in the regulation and supervision of the insurance industry and conducts periodic checks to test the robustness of the insurance companies (competing international financial center).

Recommendations for Shanghai

Much work has been done over the past year to develop a regulatory framework for health insurance business as the need to finance costs of healthcare through insurance is expected to grow tremendously with the aging population and the increasingly well-informed and more affluent public. Recognizing the market's needs for long-term health insurance services, many insurers have begun introducing products with non-cancelable and pre-funding features in recent years. As these features require long-term financial commitments to be made by consumers, it is important that the information disclosed to consumers is sufficient for them to make an informed decision on the financial commitments that they are undertaking. In addition, persons employed in distribution channels should be competent and provide sound advice on health insurance. The proposed health insurance framework, which addresses the above issues, is expected to be launched in 2004.

According to the data shown from the insurance income in Shanghai, the operation income (not including premium income) from the investment-linked insurance products was up to 0.902 billion RMB, increased by almost 37.01% in the same quarter. This kind of product accounts for almost one-third of the life-long insurance companies' total income. The potential of the invest-linked products could bring a huge implied profit for the customers, as well as providing a basic protection for those who can claim on their premium charges over death or health. The insurance industry in other counties or cities such as Hong Kong was prosperous due to these kind of diversified insurance products. It is also believed that the promotion of more diversified insurance products in investments, health, business annuity and retirement should be done, in this case with greater insurance business supervision set up in the city and stronger teams for research and development. Insurance product quality should be continuously monitored and maintained by the insurance authorities with good risk-management support.

3.3 Bonds

Current situation in Shanghai

While Asia has demonstrated remarkable resilience in face of the subprime mortgage crisis, the region was not completely spared. During the crisis, bond markets (Shanghai included) provided just 20% of the debt financing throughout the region, while banks provided the remaining 80%. At the same time in the US, bond financing accounts for as much as 60% of total debt financing. This over-reliance of banks poses a threat that if the banking sector fails, the flow of finance will be severely hindered .

Since the region is not open to other alternative financial resources, and since bank-lending is relatively short-term, businesses run the risk that new and existing loans might be cut back as was the case during the crisis where bank-lending all but collapsed and foreign banks withdrew vast amounts of capital from the financial system.

Reflections from other international financial cities

Hong Kong's bond market is the second largest in Asia behind Japan. According to the HKMA, Hong Kong's bond issuing bodies include the Exchange Fund, statutory organizations, multilateral development banks (MDB25s), non-MDB overseas banks, authorized institutions

(AI26s) and local corporations. They are all subject to certain restrictions in their bond issuing needs. Public sector bonds are the Exchange Fund Bills and Notes issued and managed by the Hong Kong Monetary Authority (HKMA). Hong Kong has pegged its dollar to the US$, making the currency convertible. Thus, the fixed income instruments issued are commonly in Hong Kong dollars. While the debt market fell into a slump after the subprime mortgage crisis, conditions in the Hong Kong have continued to improve. A record volume of Hong Kong dollar bonds were issued by non-government corporations in 2012 (Department, 2012). Better progress was also made in implementing the Government Bond Program, including a retail bond offering that set records in the retail bond market in Hong Kong.

As for Singapore, the development of debt markets has been one of the key components of the MAS's initiatives to consolidate Singapore's position as an international financial center. The debt market in Singapore is made up of three major segments: Singapore government securities (SGS24) market, the Asian dollar bond (ADB) market, and the Singapore dollar corporate bond (SDCB) market. Since Singapore and Hong Kong historically ran—and continues to run—large fiscal surpluses, and, Singapore especially, maintains huge reserves, the two cities have theoretically little need to finance their budget through the issuance of bonds or Treasury notes. Thus, the motive behind issuing government securities or bonds has been to stimulate the emergence of a debt market and to establish benchmark rates. Many financial sector analysts view the Singapore Dollar denominated bond market as promising. The issuer base is becoming more diversified, from being dominated by property companies in 1998 to a better mix of government-linked companies, statutory boards, foreign entities, and financial institutions (Ngiam & Loh, 2002). In addition, the volume of derivative transactions is also on the rise. One key constraint is the very shallow secondary market for these bonds. To date, insurance companies have been the largest buyers. With a huge appetite for fixed-income securities, they rarely trade, adopting the buy-and-hold approach. As a result, the Singapore bond market is mainly a primary market, with little secondary trading. The lack of liquidity and depth of the market are the main deterrent for foreign fund managers to invest in the market.

Recommendations for Shanghai

Reflecting upon the successes of other financial centers, a good step for Shanghai to take will be to shift some of China's government foreign currency reserves into local bond funds. The development of an active sovereign wealth bond fund would help to channel the region's wealth back into local businesses, direct savings into investment more effectively, provide protection from foreign exchange risks, reduce excessive current account surpluses and provide long-term projects with the option of longer-term borrowing. In addition, a secondary bond market should also be actively developed. Restrictions on private investors should be lifted or kept minimal while certain policies can be implemented on institutional investors such as insurance companies to prevent them from dominating the market. This will ensure greater liquidity in the bond market.

3.4 Equities and other products

Current situation in Shanghai

Although the Shanghai Stock Exchange is the largest in China, it is small compared to that of Singapore's and Hong Kong's. In addition, many regulatory frameworks of new listing and ways of attracting foreign capital have not been properly developed.

Besides equities, other financial products are also limited in quantity and poor in quality due to strict lack of financial intermediaries and strict capital requirements.

Reflections from other international financial cities

Singapore and Hong Kong stock markets are generally regarded as more established in Asia. The market capitalization for Singapore Stock Exchange is US $738.289 billion (as of 31 December 2012) and the total number of listed companies was 776 (The World Bank, 2012). The market capitalization of Singapore's securities market has increased more than 10 folds over the past 20 years, indicating that the government has been generally successful in its financial reforms and in attracting foreign capital. On the liquidity front, however, Singapore has a relatively lower trading turnover. This has been a growing concern as the capital market seems to be dragged down by the low trading volume. Reforms are therefore aimed at enhancing the liquidity of the market as well as encouraging more listings. One of them is liberalizing the use of Central Provident Fund savings, allowing citizens to use their savings for investment (San, 2004). This gave the securities market an important boost. The loosening of the listing requirements also allowed more firms to issue equities to fund their activities.

The market capitalization for Hong Kong Stock Exchange is US$2.554 trillion (as of 30 September 2012) and the total number of listed companies was 1533 (The World Bank, 2012). The Hong Kong securities and futures markets have undergone several major changes since 1997. In view of the economic integration with Mainland China, many mainland enterprises flooded to list in Hong Kong. A great degree of liquidity (compared to Singapore) coupled with little regulation allows Hong Kong to digest many huge IPOs, for example, the IPO for the Agricultural Bank of China Ltd which set the record for the world's largest IPO (Jun, Woo, & Ho, 2010). While the market capitalization of Singapore and Hong Kong pale when compared with stock markets like NYSE and LSE in terms of absolute figures, a more realistic and meaningful comparison can be drawn using market capitalization as a percentage of GDP to show how successful are the capital markets in their respective economies. Topping the list is Hong Kong where the ratio of its market capitalization to GDP is several times its annual GDP. This is perhaps the largest amongst the other developed capital markets globally.

Recommendations for Shanghai

As can be seen from the case of Singapore and Hong Kong, foreign capital is essential to the growth of the financial sector. As Shanghai aims to become a global financial center, it is important to open up its stock market to foreign companies. This, however, leads to the problem of whether to allow the Chinese Yuan to become fully convertible. The Beijing government has all along adopted a strict monetary policy which prevents the Chinese Yuan from becoming fully convertible. This has, to a large extent, shielded Shanghai from the recent financial crisis. If China were to free up its currency to the global capital market, sufficient risk management and supervision will be needed to ensure the financial stability.

Due to the absence of security lending facilities, high regulatory capital requirements, the lack of dedicated option market makers and cumbersome settlement procedures, trading of equity options in the OTC market has not taken off in Asia. There is thus an impetus for Shanghai to hasten the introduction of derivative products to take the lead in the Asian market. To meet the market demand of quality derivatives and futures, the Shanghai financial institutions should invent more diversified derivative products, with good quality and a regulation system. The investors and the developers should work together to build up market majority financing and capitalization management.

In order to achieve a healthy and dynamic environment for the currency markets, the currency market establishment is recommended to be largely expanded with better currency market management. The market currency broker service should be developed just as other financial centers such as South Korea and London, with a greater government support in the small to middle financial institutions. Other than currency markets, the commodity markets such as gold should be pushed to develop into a fully transactional service, from saving, transport, and segmentation to gold accounts.

4 Strengthening Supervision by Regulations

4.1 Goal to be achieved

Every time when there is financial crisis or speculation, the financial market in a country will be substantially influenced. In order to reduce the negative effects of these severe events, intervention from government is essential. According to the 12th 5 Year Plan of Financial Development and Reformation of China, China plans to strengthen supervision over the financial market, maintaining the market in a stable situation.

4.2 Reflections from Other International Financial Cities

The Hong Kong Monetary Authority (HKMA) is the greatest financial regulator in Hong Kong. Its objective is to ensure the stability of the HK currency and the banking system, carrying out duties such as banking supervision, monetary management, the promotion of industry integrity and development of the financial system.

Although Hong Kong is already one of the biggest financial centers in Asia, it still puts lots of effort into maintaining the strength of the international role of the HK financial center. The HK government established the Financial Services Development Council in January 2013. It is not only responsible for extending, promoting, and supervising the financial market, but also training workers to have more knowledge and ability related to financial activities.

Similarly, there is the Monetary Authority of Singapore (MAS) to oversee all areas of the Singapore financial sector. It is in charge of the supervision of banking, insurance, securities and futures industries, as well as the future development plan of Singapore as an international financial center. Moreover, it has encouraged foreign investment in its markets by removing obstacles to capital flows and constantly reviewing and improving the effectiveness of its regulatory system. Its strong legal system and low levels of corruption are also key factors that draw foreign business to this little red dot. Due to the successes of MAS, Singapore has been described by the World Bank as having the most business-friendly regulation in the world.

In recent years after the Asian Financial Crisis, Singapore shifted its regulatory emphasis from protecting the domestic banking sector to one based on supervision that was much more focused on transparency and managing systemic risk. With the aim of turning Singapore into an international finance hub, the government launched a series of financial sector reform. In May 1999, a five year liberalization plan was announced, mainly to align current regulation and supervision with international best practice (Solutions, 2011), which assumes a form of prudential supervision and disclosure-based regulation. In order to achieve its goal, Singapore has developed the necessary institutional infrastructure, as well as proficient technical capability at conducting such supervision. There is now a high level of compliance with international standards and codes of best practice for regulation and disclosure.

4.3 Recommendations for Shanghai

Instead of one big financial authority like in Singapore and Hong Kong, there are China Securities, Banking, and Insurance Regulatory Commissions for supervising financial activities in Shanghai. According to the previous descriptions, the success of Singapore as an international financial center is due to the robust regulatory infrastructure and a strong rule of law. To foster greater confidence among foreign institutions in its financial sector, Shanghai could put in place a strong rule of law and ensure that businesses are properly supervised within its jurisdictions. Furthermore, given that the financial regulation in both Hong Kong and Singapore is mainly carried out by a single chief regulator (HKMA and MAS), China government should consider establishing a lead agency that co-ordinates all regulatory activities. Then financial market in Shanghai might be in a more stable situation without huge fluctuations.

However, as can be seen from the current challenges faced by Singapore, Shanghai needs to avoid being over reliant on the rule-based, compliance-led approach. While basic rules are necessary, Shanghai should aim to move towards a model of principles-based legislation, one which encourages senior management within financial institutions to assume greater responsibility in ensuring the legitimacy of company actions. While a purely rule-based approach will tend to encourage organizations to regard conforming to international standards as a task to be performed by their compliance departments, a principles-based approach will better allow senior management to try to assimilate these standards into their daily operations.

5 Development of Modern Business and Communications Infrastructure

5.1 Goals to be achieved

Efficient, reliable, and modern infrastructure services are not only crucial for attracting investment and increasing international competitiveness, but serve to boost economic growth and job creation.

In addition to necessities such as affordable and modern office space, stable and reliable sources of power generation (electricity, natural gas), the widespread availability of robust telecommunications, an efficient transportation system, a clean and adequate water supply, and sanitation services are among the important components of an attractive infrastructure. By contrast, insufficient roads, ports and power generation all can act as chokepoints that diminish the attractiveness and economic potential of an economy. Moreover, these bottlenecks can even negate a country's significant low production cost advantage.

5.2 Current situation in Shanghai

Shanghai has focused on developing its physical infrastructure since the 1990s, and many of these projects were finished before the World Exposition.

Shanghai has two world-class international airports, the world's busiest port and longest metro network, which includes the world's first maglev train. Hosting two "super tall" skyscrapers: Shanghai World Financial Center (492 m) and Jin Mao Tower (421 m), Shanghai also has one of the largest number of office buildings among all IFCs. This shows the world that Shanghai is now ready to evolve into an international financial center. However, currently, only 3.3% of Shanghai's population works in the financial services industry, half the percentage of that in New York, Tokyo, London and Hong Kong. While this may seem to be a large margin, experience from the European Union does tell that human capital moves quickly with globalization (Heinz & Ward-Warmedinger, 2006). In fact, the number of foreign financial services employees in Shanghai has doubled during 2003-2009, reaching 150,000.

5.3 Reflections from Other International Financial Cities

Hong Kong has a superb business infrastructure system. The strong infrastructure support meets its population's needs and contributes to growth of the economy as well as financial development. In the first case, Hong Kong has an advanced land, sea, and air transport and communications system. These include efficient and convenient local and regional transport, world-class telecommunications and connectivity and world-leading sea and air cargo systems. For example, the huge project launched in 2001 constructed 6 more lines to facilitate the rail traffic between Hong Kong Island and the rest of the territory. These lead to greater freight links with mainland China to meet the expected future needs in business and financial exchange.

To penetrate further, let us first take a look on its international connectivity around the world. A good international connectivity indicates good business transactions and communications between countries, as Hong Kong is always the location of world-class financial conventions and exhibitions. For business travelers, flights are available for more than 180 cities around the world, including at least 48 locations in Mainland China, with flight service markets still rapidly expanding. In this case, Hong Kong International Airport is one of the world's busiest international airports and also the hub of many international airlines which include China. Now the Hong Kong government plans to construct the 3rd railway before 2017 to prevent the saturation of the system capacity.

As a reference for Shanghai, Hong Kong also possesses an excellent telecom infrastructure to facilitate the financial exchange between countries and regions. The telecom infrastructure is at a very affordable rate, with the broadband and 3G networks covering almost the whole territory. The fast accessible internet and mobile phone service allows users to have first-hand financial information in the markets, with mere short delays of information and updated news from around the world. In addition, the mass media conduct their news in different channels with international languages including Mandarin and English subtitles and translation provided.

In Singapore, the telecommunications infrastructure spans the entire city-state. The whole island is closely accessible to the Singapore population and the inhabited parts. According to the Singapore government statistics, there were more than 4.8 million broadband users all over Singapore in 2009. Radio and television stations are all government-owned and the broadcast signals could be picked up from Malaysia and Indonesia at the same time due to proximity in regions. As for the print media section, Singapore Press Holdings manages to hold the newspaper markets and all the daily newspapers are published in 4 languages including Chinese, English, Malay and Tamil. The language accessibility is high for different personnel in financial institutions and the daily news of all financial channels such as Bloomberg is also easily-accessible for all the businessmen and the citizens.

5.4 Recommendations for Shanghai

This part focuses on the development of the business and communications infrastructure in the city. It is advised that the development of Shanghai's urban internal and external transport system should be highly emphasized in the coming couple of years to meet the demand for financial and communication exchange.

With regard to the internal land transportation, Shanghai already provides a good network for citizens to travel inside the city. However, in the coming years, the Metro railway system should be further expanded to penetrate to the outward circles of the city. This allows more people to get in and out of the financial hub in the city with fast and convenient service. This is accompanied by the target of "153060" which indicates the success of a shorter travel time and easier conventions. A side advantage could be a relief for the public transportation burden which is suffered by the citizens every day especially in peak working hours.

Shanghai has a unique and advantageous geographical position in Mainland China and this could help Shanghai be an international financial exchange center. It is the government suggested that invest more money in improving the port facilities and airport infrastructure, with the addition of safety concerns. This could help attract more businessmen to consider Shanghai as a safe and convenient place to hold international exhibitions and financial transactions. The service quality in the airports should be strictly scrutinized, with promise of less delay of air flights and strict supervision of airplane conditions by the engineers. Due to the increase traffic capacity, the airport should prepare reports regularly to see if it needs the expansion of space or building of extra railways. The collaboration with more airlines of different cities around the world is a must for a good financial exchange.

Lastly, in terms of telecommunications, Shanghai could be more advanced and taking up a more vigorous role in this aspect. The expansion of good-quality 3G network service and accessibility of free-provided Wi-Fi service in public places such as libraries and restaurants could be further emphasized. The business media is highly encouraged to give us information in the open financial and business markets and transactions with multi-language coverage. The government is encouraged to open up new business channels, as well as business and financial press focusing on local and international financial industry updates and news.

6 Building and Education of Human Capital and Financial Talents

Goals to be achieved

People are of increasing importance, especially in emerging markets. A research conducted by the Corporation of London found that the availability of skilled personnel was the most important competitive factor for building a financial center. The availability of a large and continually renewed skilled and educated workforce is a key to the development and long-term survival of world-class financial centers that depend on advanced technology and constant innovation. The expertise of its workforce is the fundamental driver of the performance and competitiveness of the financial services industry. Therefore, How to attract, maintain and develop more financial talents to Shanghai has always been the main concern of financial centers so as to enhance the internationalization of the domestic capital market.

Reflections from Other International Financial Cities

The Capital Investment Entrant Scheme (CIES) was implemented in October 2003 to allow capital investment entrants, i.e. persons who make capital investments, to reside in Hong Kong without establishing, joining or running a business. It may seem logical to conclude that when the CIES investment threshold was raised from HK$6.5 million to HK$10 million in October 2010, investors would be turned off. On the contrary, Hong Kong received 16,600 entrant applications. Out of these, 8,924 applicants had already made the requisite investments, which totaled approximately HK$63.31 billion and were granted approval to reside in the territory.

The above-mentioned data only points us away from the perception that Hong Kong's migration policies are impediments to business. Today, countries around the world are waking up to the fact that highly-talented professionals and entrepreneurial investors are mobile. A country's economic prosperity is inextricably linked to its immigration policy; a case in point being Singapore. Singapore has long been known as Hong Kong's key competitor in the region and has been steadily attracting investments, foreign capital and talented professionals. One of the key factors driving the economy forward is its open immigration policy. There is no denying that the open-door policy is a red hot political issue attracting criticism from the local community, but the reality is that it has worked to Singapore's advantage.

Recommendations for Shanghai

To establish human capital, especially for the financial industry, where the competition in the global market for well-trained and qualified professionals is especially acute, quality of life has become a key consideration for attracting and retaining international employees. As a result, beyond reliable and modern infrastructure such as electricity, water, air and ground transportation, commercial office space, and telecommunications, world class medical care, superior educational opportunities for financial professionals' children, proximate housing and physical security, as well as access to sophisticated leisure activities, are also extremely important.

Besides, flexible Labor Laws to attract a skilled workforce is significant as is the decision by financial services firms to locate in a particular place. This is directly linked to the depth of the pool of skilled workers across the full range of their hiring needs (from sophisticated post-graduates to office workers) that is available there. This also needs to include their freedom under local law to manage their business, including reasonable business flexibility to hire and dismiss employees.

World-class financial centers possess secondary and university education systems that produce graduates of the highest quality in fields essential to financial innovation: e.g., mathematics, economics and information technology. Moreover, a large and continually growing pool of qualified graduates is necessary to develop and maintain the critical mass of accountants, auditors, lawyers, and other personnel who support sophisticated and innovative financial firms.

Every world-class financial center draws a significant amount of its human capital from the local labor market. Attracting, but also maintaining, the best talent is critical to the creation of a world-class financial center. Consequently, labor laws that permit flexible hiring and dismissal of workers are a critically important feature of such a center. Inflexible labor markets stifle job creation, and can deter foreign investment. Moreover, inflexible labor markets impede the ability of firms to adjust to changes in the economic environment as a result of new technologies, economic shocks, and the impact of trade agreements.

Increasing product diversification can attract sophisticated international investors and with more and more job opportunity and relevant policies providing incentives, the financial skilled workforce will inevitably shift. The A-share market has been stopped allowing the company listed for a year. Many companies chose Hong Kong to IPO. With more IPO opportunities and therefore job opportunities attracting talent, it can create synergies for building its status as a financial center.

Furthermore, behind that phenomenon of skilled labor movement, immigration policy plays an important role. Like in Singapore, with loose immigration policies targeting financial professionals, the statistics show the increase in population, and it is recommended to increase communication between different government departments and formulate better immigration policy. Immigration policy has to be relaxed in order to provide the first fertile soil for this big financial tree to grow and cultivate the local financial talents by referring the immigration policy in Hong Kong and Singapore. The connectivity between the major financial markets will be enhanced by the increased mobility of the professionals.

7 Limitations

Since China's financial market is much bigger compared to other countries or regions, it is hard for the insurance commission to supervise all insurance products' quality. Although Shanghai has great potential to develop an insurance market, the problem of supervision over all the insurance products must exist.

In addition, for the goal of one great financial authority, each part of financial sector has its own law and regulation, so it is hard to have one great authority to supervise or control other smaller commissions.

Last but not least, since there are many countries with developed financial sector in Asia, it will be hard work to compare all of them and Shanghai.

8   Conclusions

Stepping into the 21st century, the status and position of international finance are becoming increasingly important worldwide. It could be easily inferred from the report that there are many developed international financial hubs in the world, including America, European countries and Asian financial cities such as Hong Kong, Taiwan and Singapore. Great financial operations and businesses could bring many opportunities for both government and citizens to generate wealth and income.

These years, developing a financial city especially Shanghai in China is recognized to possess potential and strength to be further developed in the next twenty years into a mature international financial center in Asia. As quoted in the report of 12th 5 Year Plan of Financial Development and Reformation, Shanghai is set to achieve the target of powerful financial development by the government's push and people's financial awareness. Therefore clear goals should be set in order to achieve future reformation.

We have conducted some studies and formulated some suggestions through various research approaches. To achieve a desired financial position in Asia, Shanghai has a unique geographical position and human talents as its advantages for financial developments. Since its position in Asia has proximity to other Asian financial cities, especially Hong Kong and Singapore, we have made the most of the references from these two locations and got some valuable insights through them. We have focused our report in four parts, which are the four targets needed to be achieved for Shanghai in the coming years.

First, we want Shanghai to be developed as a market center possessing diversified quality financial products. The great importance lies primarily on the equity markets, including stocks and bonds from different parties. As Shanghai aims to become a global financial center, it is important to first open up its stock market to foreign companies from different counties. Shanghai could take a further step by shifting some of China's government foreign currency reserves into local bond funds. It is recommended that the currency market establishment be largely expanded with better currency market management. Other commodity products like gold and derivatives should be largely invented by the authorized and carefully-hired research and development teams.

Secondly strict monetary and financial regulations should be exercised by a powerful government body. Shanghai is advised to set up a single chief regulator such as HKMA monitoring all the financial institutions in Shanghai, the securities exchange, the central government financial policies and the cash flows. At the same time, the regulations and rules of different financial sectors should be revised regularly. These include the procedures of security issues, financial contract terms, insurance policies and other important financial exchange such as commodity, gold and derivatives. Strict penalties should be enforced to avoid any illegal transactions and market control since they will easily influence the market price and state of inflation or deflation.

The third point to be noted is the sophisticated development of business and telecommunications infrastructure. According to the examples of other developed financial cities such as Tokyo, New York and Singapore, they all have two features in common, i.e. a sophisticated and convenient transportation network and telecommunications system for facilitating business communications and financial information exchange. Shanghai is advised to put more effort in building a sophisticated transportation network system reaching out to different business areas in Shanghai, with more advanced and complete facilities and signaling systems. The airport should be further developed into a world-recognized one with great quality service and better worldwide linkage to other cities. The telecommunications system, including telephone, cellphone and wireless access should be further improved in quality and more hotspots should be provided to different business locations. The television, newspapers and press are advised to open more financial channels and information proliferation which are done by the collaborative effort of the media and the government itself.

Lastly, Shanghai should put more efforts into financial human capital and talent building. Shanghai could take reference from Hong Kong's talent immigration policy and put more emphasis on the education qualities in tertiary education and business-related subjects. More exchange programs, international exhibitions and financial conferences could be held in order to facilitate communications and learning among the students and the business talents.

If Shanghai government could follow the above four main targets, though with limitations such as inadequate human capital and government control policies, it could be believed Shanghai could be largely developed and becomes a mature and international financial center in the near future.

References

The World Bank. (2012). *Market Capitalization of Listed Companies (% of GDP)*. Available at http: //data.worldbank.org/indicator/CM.MKT.LCAP.GD.ZS

Cainey, A. (2010). *Shanghai Building an International Financial Center with Chinese Characteristics.* Perspective. Available at http: //wenku.baidu.com/view/3407d50bba1aa8114431d9df.html

Monetary Management Department. (2012). *The Hong Kong Debt Market in 2012.* Available at http: //www.hkma.gov.hk/media/eng/publication-and-research/quarterly-bulletin/qb201303/fa1.pdf

Huat, T. C., Lim, J., and Chen, W. (2004). *Competing International Financial Centers: A Comparative Study between Hong Kong and Singapore.* Singapore.

IMF. (2013). *Data Template on International Reserves and Foreign Currency Liquidity*. Available at http: //www.imf.org/external/np/sta/ir/IRProcessWeb/colist.aspx

Luo, J., Woo, E., and Ho, C. K. (2010). *Agricultural Bank of China Sets IPO Record as Size Raised to $22.1 Billion*. Available at http: //www.bloomberg.com/news/2010-08-15/agricultural-bank-of-china-sets-ipo-record-with-22-1-billion-boosted-sale.html.

Ngiam, K. J., and Loh, L. (2002). Developing debt market in Singapore: rationale, challenges and prospects. *Asia-Pacific Development Journal*, 9(1).

Piotroski, J. D., Wong, T. J. (2011). Institutions and Information Environment of Chinese Listed Firms. The Chinese University of Hong Kong, Hong Kong. Available at http: //www.baf.cuhk.edu.hk/research/ief/documents/book/capitalizing_china_05.pdf

Republic, Research. (2008). *The Future of Asian Financial Centers — Challenges and Opportunities for the City of London*.

San, T. S. (2004). *The Central Provident Fund: More Than Retirement*. Available at http: //www.cscollege.gov.sg/Knowledge/Ethos/Ethos%20July%202004/Pages/The%20Central%20Provident%20Fund%20More%20Than%20Retirement.aspx.

Solutions, J. C. (2011). Banking Industry and Major Banks in Singapore. Available at http: //www.guidemesingapore.com/doing-business/finances/singapore-banking-industry-overview

WCC. (2008). *World Competitiveness Yearbook*. Available at http: //www.imd.org/wcc/.

Appendices

1. GFCI 13 ranks and ratings

Table 1 GFCI 13 ranks and ratings

Centre	GFCI 13		GFCI 12		CHANGES	
	Rank	Rating	Rank	Rating	Rank	Rating
London	1	807	1	785	—	▲ 22

APPROACHES AND CHALLENGES

continued

Centre	GFCI 13		GFCI 12		CHANGES	
	Rank	Rating	Rank	Rating	Rank	Rating
New York	2	787	2	765	—	▲ 22
Hong Kong	3	761	3	733	—	▲ 28
Singapore	4	759	4	725	—	▲ 34
Zurich	5	723	5	691	—	▲ 32
Tokyo	6	718	7	684	▲ 1	▲ 34
Geneva	7	712	9	682	▲ 2	▲ 30
Boston	8	711	11	680	▲ 3	▲ 31
Seoul	9	710	6	685	-3	▲ 25
Frankfurt	10	703	13	677	▲ 3	▲ 26
Chicago	11	698	8	683	-3	▲ 15
Toronto	12	696	10	681	-2	▲ 15
San Francisco	13	695	12	678	-1	▲ 17
Washington D.C.	14	692	14	672	—	▲ 20
Vancouver	15	690	16	668	▲ 1	▲ 22
Montreal	16	689	17	667	▲ 1	▲ 22
Calgary	17	688	23	647	▲ 6	▲ 41
Luxembourg	18	687	24	646	▲ 6	▲ 41
Sydney	19	686	15	670	-4	▲ 16
Vienna	20	685	36	633	▲ 16	▲ 52

continued

	GFCI 13		GFCI 12		CHANGES	
Centre	Rank	Rating	Rank	Rating	Rank	Rating
Kuala Lumpur	21	681	26	644	▲ 5	▲ 37
Osaka	22	676	21	650	-1	▲ 26
Dubai	23	675	22	648	-1	▲ 27
Shanghai	24	674	19	656	-5	▲ 18
Melbourne	25	672	18	657	-7	▲ 15

2. Ranking of Foreign Exchange Reserves

Rank	Country	Foreign Exchange Reserves (Millions of US$)	Figures as of
1	People's Republic of China	3,341,000	Dec 2012[1]
2	Japan	1,238,713	Jun 2013[2]
3	Eurozone	808,192	May 2013[2]
4	Saudi Arabia	656,900	Dec 2012[1]
5	Russia	518,431	May 2013[2]

(IMF 2013)

3. Developing path of building up human capital

Chapter 3

Building the International Financial Center: Path and Highlights for Shanghai

Rujia Wang [1], Xina Liu [2], Xiaokai Jin [3], Yashu Li [4]
Shanghai Finance University Team
Coach: Wanpeng Cheng[*]

Shanghai was long regarded as the financial center of the Asia-Pacific before 1937. Although it suffered from several disasters, e.g. Sino-Japanese War, Chinese Civil War, "the Cultural Revolution", a series of supporting policies were put forward to recover its old-time glory since 1978, when China's Reform and Openness began. Fortunately, it has yielded fruit in terms of the number and range of financial institutions.

In this report, we firstly note Shanghai's relative advantages and disadvantages compared with other International Financial centers (IFCs hereafter). As a famous harbor in China, Shanghai is endowed

---

[1] Rujia Wang is an undergraduate majoring in credit management at Shanghai Finance University.
[2] Xina Liu is an undergraduate majoring in finance at Shanghai Finance University.
[3] Xiaokai Jin is an undergraduate majoring in international trade and economics at Shanghai Finance University.
[4] Yashu Li is an undergraduate majoring in international business at Shanghai Finance University.
[*] Wangpeng Cheng is an Assistant Professor in School of International Finance at Shanghai Finance University. He earned his doctorate in economics from Chonbuk National University. His research interests focus on International Finance.

with superior natural conditions and China's growing economic backing behind. On the other hand, its weaknesses should not be ignored. So far, compared with Hong Kong and London, Shanghai still has a long way to go.

Next, we focus on the problems existing in the construction of Shanghai IFC, discussing the problems of human capital, infrastructure and regulation. Frankly, Shanghai lacks high-level financial talents compared with other IFCs. In addition, it's supposed that there still will be a huge upgrade for Shanghai in terms of regulation and infrastructure. Following the problems we put forward, we will discuss government's necessary contribution to improve market efficiency in China.

Finally, with reflection on those issues we have mentioned, we will provide feasible approaches to Shanghai's further IFC construction.

1 Financial History of Shanghai

Phase 1: Pre-1937

The prosperous financial history of pre-1937 China largely focused on one city — Shanghai. The reason is that it is located at the juncture of Huangpu River and Yangtze River, right before the latter joins the Pacific Ocean. What's more, Shanghai opened to British for trade and settlement under the provisions of the Treaty of Nanjing signed in 1843, followed by the establishment of the French Concession in 1849.

Following China's compelled -openness, numerous foreign institutions poured in. In 1930s, Shanghai had been developed indisputably as the Asia-Pacific's finance center. In 1934, Shanghai, which was viewed as the "Paris of the East", hosted 33 foreign banks, more than Hong Kong (21) and Singapore (17), 24 state banks and over 200 private lenders, trust companies and other financial institutions. Along with London and New York, Shanghai also hosted one of the largest stock markets in the world.

Phase 2: From 1937 to 1978

Shanghai's fall also came quickly. Global currency crisis, wartime inflation and Sino-Japanese War pushed bankers, entrepreneurs and financiers out of Shanghai to Hong Kong, Taiwan or overseas. Furthermore, China was shut off from the outside world in 1949 and, what's worse to Shanghai, financial institutions were collectively relocated to Beijing. From 1956 to 1978, Shanghai's development was directed to follow the Soviet model of heavy industry. Impractical political and economic policies nationwide also severely impacted Shanghai's economy and infrastructure.

On the other side, Tokyo, Hong Kong, Singapore and other cities developed rapidly and secured their leading positions in global economy during that time.

Phase 3: From 1978 to present

Devastated during the past forty years, Shanghai was eager for recovering its old-time state as the Asia-Pacific's financial center. Therefore, from 1978 onwards, Shanghai government has put forward a series of supporting policies and established a large number of financial institutions.

Supporting policies

Reform and Open Policy

At the turning point, the influence of Reform and Opening-up Policy implemented in 1978 was of the greatest significance. Since then, Shanghai's economic development has been concentrating on the tertiary sector and foreign trade. The tertiary sector (1,114.286 billion RMB in 2011) has gained a dominant position in Shanghai's economy, accounting for 58% of GDP in 2011, compared with China's average level of 43.1%. Wholesale and retail industries and financial industry made the top two subsectors, with the latter's value reaching 2.274 billion RMB in 2011.

Economic Reform in Pudong District

In 1990, Shanghai was granted some privileges in China's second-round economic reforms, including developing the Pudong District and constructing a Special Economic Zone (SEZ). The building of Lujiazui Financial Trade Zone, Jinqiao Export Processing Zone and Waigaoqiao Free Trade Zone symbolized the beginning of a package of policy reforms. This visionary strategy, appealed to worldwide capital and technology, was preliminarily consistent with the construction of the IFC. Since 1992, Shanghai's economic growth rate has surpassed national average level and has been growing 12% annually on average.

First RMB cross-border settlement

China's State Council announced a pilot program in April, 2009 to allow exporters and importers in Shanghai to settle cross-border trade deals in China's currency — RMB. It was a significant step toward totally free settlement of RMB against other currencies. The first cross-border RMB settlement deal was made between Shanghai and Hong Kong, which showed China central government's intention of strengthening financial cooperation between Shanghai and Hong Kong to boost mutual development of financial sectors of such two metropolises. This trial could largely protect traders against fluctuation in exchange rates, simplify settlement procedures and reduce transaction cost, even defend against potential currency crisis.

IFC construction plan

In March 2009, China's State Council announced an ambitious plan of turning Shanghai into "an international financial center" in correspondence with the size of China's economy and the RMB's international position in 2020. The ambition aimed to make Shanghai a world-class leading IFC, and make it competitive with London and New York by 2020. The announcement significantly marked, a concrete national-level backing and authorization of Shanghai's future status. Prior to then, Shanghai only functioned as China's domestic financial center and there was little difference between Shanghai and Beijing and Shenzhen.

Shanghai Free Trade Zone(FTZ)

The State Council approved Shanghai Free Trade Zone Plan on

July 3, 2013. The plan encompassed an area of 28 square kilometers, including Waigaoqiao Free Trade Zone, Yangshan Free Trade Port Area and Pudong Airport Comprehensive Free Trade Zone. This giant program will take more than 10 years to be completed. Shanghai FTZ will allow goods' import, processing, delivery and export free of duties. What's more, investors will be allowed to conduct multi-currency finance trade including free transactions between RMB and other foreign currencies within it, actually much similar to a local offshore financial market settled in Shanghai. It is expected that this plan will attract more global companies, especially those in the tertiary sector, to establish their Asia-Pacific headquarters in the Shanghai in near future.

Financial institutions

The table given below illustrates major financial institutions established in Shanghai since 1990. We can recognize from the table that Shanghai is trying to construct a multifaceted IFC in an all-round way.

So far, all Chinese national commercial banks have set numerous branches in Shanghai. On Aug 10th, 2005, the second headquarter of China's central bank, People's Bank of China, was established in Shanghai, representing the central government's ambition to promote Shanghai finance industry. The HSBC Group, Standard Chartered, Citibank Group, BEA, Hang Seng Bank, DBS, as well as many other world famous institutions established their local headquarters in Shanghai which show their confidence in Shanghai IFC construction.

Table 1-1 Financial Institutions in Shanghai since 1990

Financial Institutions	Content	Year	State or Scale
Shanghai Securities Exchange	Main capital market (equity, bonds)	1990	80 per cent of total trading turnover in China

continued

Financial Institutions	Content	Year	State or Scale
Foreign Exchange Trading center	Foreign exchange	1994	Head office of national trading market
Inter-bank Loan center	Money market	1996	National center for interbank trading
RMB Bond Trading center	Money market	1997	National center for bond trading
Shanghai Futures Exchange	Rubber, copper, aluminum and fuel oil	1999	60 per cent of futures trading volume of all China
Shanghai Gold Exchange	Gold market	2002	The only gold market
Shanghai Petroleum Market	Futures Transactions	2006	The only petroleum market in China
China Financial Futures Exchange	Financial derivative transactions	2006	The only derivative market in China

Source: Young *et al*. (eds.) (2009: 234)

As of 2011, Shanghai has become the largest commercial and financial center of mainland China, hosting 160 banks, 333 insurance providers and 149 security institutions. Among the total 1,048 financial institutions, 173 are foreign entities.

2 Shanghai's Relative Advantages and Disadvantages Compared with Other IFCs

2.1 Strength

Shanghai is located in the east of China, endowed with superior natural conditions. It is a dynamic city under the process of developing towards a future international financial center, which is also considered one of the most promising IFCs in the world. Moreover, the growth of China provides an advantaged developing background.

Geographical conditions

Shanghai is adjacent to the Pacific Ocean, which makes Shanghai the most famous harbor in China. Given this very convenient geographical condition, Shanghai attracts much more international investment and trade than any other city in China.

Development vision

As an IFC under construction, Shanghai faces numerous domestic opportunities. Along with the rise of Chinese economy, Shanghai benefits a lot and capture opportunities overseas. According to the result of a questionnaire from global financial centers, Index 13, Shanghai received the second-most votes from the respondents, who were asked which centers they consider likely to become more significant in the next few years. What's more, in the Xinhua-Dow Jones International Financial Centers Development Index (IFCD) released in 2012, Shanghai ranked the 1st place in the term of "growth and development", which is identical to the number in 2011.

Access to the huge and growing Chinese financial market

There is no doubt that access to the huge and growing Chinese financial market is a considerable advantage of Shanghai. First, China has over 30-years of a stable and economically oriented political environment which acts as a fundamental developing background. Second, the growth of the Chinese economy is constantly rapid, with an annual growth rate of around 10% since the Reform and Openness in 1978.

Politically stable

China has neither coup nor national turbulence for a relatively long time. More valued is its smooth transfer of authorities of latest three generations convincing worldwide investor of its long-term political stability in the future.

Macroeconomic stability

Chinese CPI is relatively reasonable in recent years, although it is under a process of mild increasing. The figure below shows changes of Chinese CPI in last 12 months.

Figure 2-1 Chinese CPI: 2012.7-2013.07(assume the same month of last year on apar with 100)

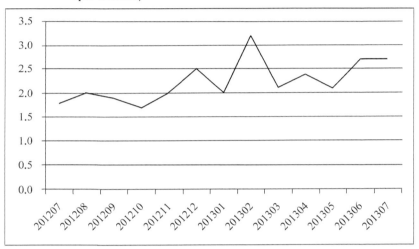

Source: National Bureau of Statistic of China

The unemployment rate is relatively tolerable in recent years in China. In the case of Shanghai, the unemployment rate was 4.35% in 2010, a bit higher than the number in 2009, but much lower than that in 2006. In general, the unemployment rate is maintaining a stable stage. Balance of payment and growth of economy of the country also have prominent past and promising future.

2.2 Weakness

Insufficient innovative capability

Compared with foreign competitors, the creativity of indigenous financial institutions in Shanghai is insufficient. The number of financial intermediate business indicates the creativity of Shanghai's financial markets to some extent. While the number of intermediate of foreign banks goes to 20,000, the corresponding number of Shanghai is poorly a few hundreds. Foreign banks benefit a lot from high-value-added activities, while Chinese banks still largely rely on the interest spread between savings and loans.

Service industry

Investment banks need access to various supporting services, such as law counseling and accounting advising. Therefore, the GFCI system ranks "access to suppliers of professional services" as the tenth most important element. However, as to the supporting service of Chinese financial system, there still will be a considerable room for upgrading.

2.3 Comparison with Hong Kong and London

Relative competitiveness

According to the GFCI[1] 13 released in March this year, London and Hong Kong ranked the first and third place respectively. What we should pay attention to is that Hong Kong ranks as the highest among all Asian cities. So there are many lessons that Shanghai can learn from Hong Kong. Also, London's success may give Shanghai right guidance on setting targets and some other macroscopic visions.

Compared with GFCI 12 released last year, Shanghai's ranking decreased 5 places from 19 to 24 this year, but the score rose from 656 to 674. At the same time, a significant rise in the score is accorded to Hong Kong and London, while their rankings are unchanged.

As a whole, on the way to becoming a well-recognized IFC, Shanghai still has a long way to go. So Shanghai should learn the practical

---

[1] The Global Financial Centres Index (GFCI) is a ranking of the competitiveness of finance centers based on over 26,000 finance center assessments from an online questionnaire together with over 80 indices from organizations such as the World Bank, the Organization for Economic Co-operation and Development (OECD) and the Economist Intelligence Unit. It is compiled and published twice a year by Z/Yen Group and sponsored by the Qatar Financial Centre Authority.

experiences from well-developed financial centers and figure out the way which is most suitable and beneficial to its own development.

Figure 2-2 Top Four Financial Centers GFCI Ratings over Time

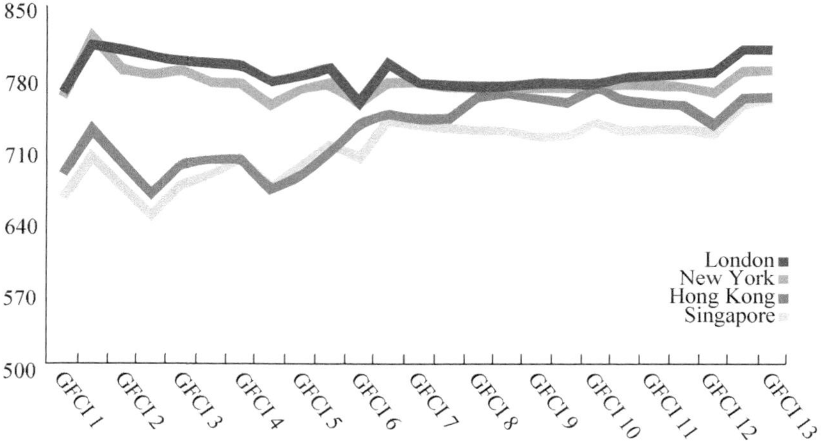

Source: GFCI report 13

Table 2-1 The Scores and Rankings of Shanghai, Hong Kong and London

City	Shanghai		Hong Kong		London	
	rank	score	Rank	score	Rank	score
GFCI 12	19	656	3	733	1	807
GFCI 13	24	674	3	761	1	785
CHANGE	-5	+18	-	+22	-	+22

Source: GFCI report 13

Talent pool

Compared with London and Hong Kong, where local people can speak English well, Shanghai lacks English-speaking staffs. As is known to all, nowadays English is a critical international tool by which one can communicate with people from different countries. Shanghai also lacks high qualified talents. In London, 15% of employed citizens have a job working in the financial system. The corresponding percentage goes to

14% in Hong Kong, compared with Shanghai's 2.2% only. Among these people, 65% of them are college graduates, less than 20% master a foreign language, and only 0.3% have got international qualifications in Shanghai.

Openness

Although openness is not listed in the GFCI report, it is still significant to the development of an international financial center. Lack of high-level openness will lessen the value of high quality financial profession, expertise, and specialized knowledge introduced into China. Openness definitely will make Shanghai as well as China benefit a lot.

Trade barriers were significantly reduced since China joined WTO in 2001. Foreign companies are more willing to do business with Chinese corporations. Under gradually serious competition from foreign corporations, Shanghai's enterprises have improved their competitiveness by improving the innovation and quality of services in the past decade. Not only can successful experience be learned, but also the lessons of failure.

Hong Kong is a convictive example for Shanghai. It is a free trade area, where there's no tariff and trade barrier, which makes it very convenient for foreign companies to do business, bringing about trade and increasing the overall competitiveness of Hong Kong the in the world.

The U.K. is a member of the European Union, which is a customs union and implements common foreign trade policy. There is no tariff or quotas between EU members, which helps U.K.'s trade value increase to a considerable value.

Corruption level

According to Transparency International Corruption Report 2012, China ranks the 80th place among 176 countries with a score of 39. Hong Kong ranks the 14th place and gets a score of 77. The rank of United Kingdom is 17 with score of 74. Compared with Hong Kong and U.K., the corruption level of China is extremely high. It is well known that the Independent Commission Against Corruption (ICAC) of Hong Kong plays an important role in successfully fighting against corruption. China's government should take actions to clean the trading environment of financial markets considering market transparency as the cornerstone of modern finance world. Within a

3 Some Existing Prominent Problems

3.1 Problem of Human Capital

What is Human Capital?

Wikipedia defines Human Capital as follows: "Human Capital is the stock of competencies, knowledge, social and personality attributes, including creativity, embodied in the ability to perform labor so as to produce economic value. It is an aggregate economic view of the human being acting within economies, which is an attempt to capture the social, biological, cultural and psychological complexity as they interact in explicit and/or economic transactions."

When we have a good understanding of what human capital is, we can continue to probe into next question. What kind of impact does human capital have on the development of an international financial center?

Relationship between Human Capital and competitiveness of IFC

Figure 3-1 Human Capital Versus Overall Competitiveness

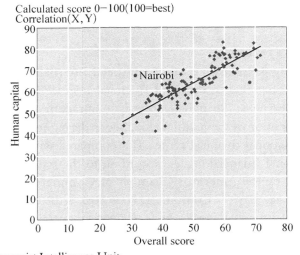

Source: Economist Intelligence Unit

Many firms fight to attract highly educated and skilled workers, and as such, many choose new cities for growth on the basis of potentially available talent pool located there. An ongoing shift towards a more knowledge-oriented economy is exacerbating this process, meaning that human capital plays a key role in the relative competitiveness of IFC.

Figure 3-1 shows a clear correlation between human capital and overall competitiveness, highlighting the importance of talent. In advanced economies, the availability of skilled labor becomes much more important and the attractiveness of the very city becomes much more important than ever before.

As a result, in the human capital dimension, emerging market cities clearly underperform. Shanghai ranked as 43rd, while Beijing was even ahead of Shanghai in this report, which ranked as 39th. It is not an easy job to attract or train proportional amounts of skilled workers specialized in the financial industry, considering huge investments has already been invested in finance-related education particularly, such as can be seen in Shanghai and other regional metropolis in China. Collecting high quality institutions and sufficiently competitive environments to attract highly skilled workers is difficult long-term work.

Shanghai's reality

There is a big gap between other advanced international financial centers and Shanghai in terms of financial talent. Compared with other domestic cities, Shanghai succeeds in attracting financial talent with obvious improvement still needed, considering its target to be a future international financial center. But compared with the target of an international financial center, according to the report "Achieving 2020" issued by the American Chamber of Commerce in Shanghai and its Financial Services Committee, New York is the most successful international financial center, with 770,000 financial professionals, Hong Kong has over 350,000 financial professionals. In contrast, the talent pool of Shanghai only has around 200,000 according to this report. Let's look at another important valuing criterion. Generally, as a worldwide international financial center, more than 10% of the population engages in the financial industry. At present the ration in Shanghai is only 1%. Therefore, promoting financial professionals, as well as their career development, is a challenging matter for Shanghai's international financial center advancement.

In December 2011, the Bureau of Shanghai Municipal Human Resources and Social Security released the Shanghai's next five-year plan for talent development. The plan calls for attracting top worldwide talent to work here and developing its local talent pool to be competitive globally. By 2015, Shanghai plans to have 320,000 financial professionals, up from 230,000 today, and 130,000 workers employed in the international shipping industry.

To attract highly qualified foreign professionals, Shanghai plans to improve the city's living environment, including developing advanced medical, cultural, and educational services, as well as subsidizing education of foreign professionals' children and providing other incentives. Shanghai is now trying a new education cooperation pattern with the help of New York University to introduce modern educational philosophy in local systems, which is supposed to be a great test for further educational reform. It is expected that Shanghai will build a talent base that drives the successful development of the city as a future IFC.

Summary

There is still much to be done to make Shanghai the place that talented financial professionals wish to work and live for reasons beyond pure career advancement. The 2012 survey by the Economist Intelligence Unit ranked Shanghai at 43rd among the cities it surveyed. According to its report, problems appear to exist in terms of many areas, including the basic living environment, air quality, education, and healthcare. For local workers, there is an acute issue of housing affordability, although this is largely a consequence of relatively low wages compared to other financial centers in the world. But this is also an offsetting advantage for firms who employ them. Real estate prices in absolute terms remain fairly low by global standards, although general laborers are suffering from higher real estate prices in the past few years.Nevertheless, it still remains fairly low in light of the global average in absolute terms. Although it is difficult to compare living costs for immigrants on a uniform basis around the world, it appears that Shanghai lags behind London and New York in terms of living costs, suggesting Shanghai still has a relative advantage situation against other advanced IFCs.

3.2 Infrastructure & Regulation

The most problematic factors, infrastructure and regulation

Figure 3-2 The Most Problematic Factors for Doing Business in Shanghai

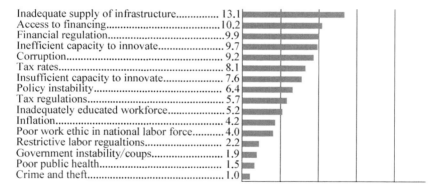

From Figure 3-2 of research outcome by Klaus Schwab above, we can draw the conclusion that the inadequate supply of infrastructure is undoubtedly blocking Shanghai's international financial center development. Global financial institutions require a huge amount of physical infrastructure to work sufficiently, including electricity, telecommunications, running water. The GFCI survey shows "availability of business infrastructure" as the fourth most important factor. If we broaden the definition of infrastructure including transportation, the ranking of it would certainly rise.

On the other hand, we cannot overlook the fact that the regulation also plays a big role in the construction of Shanghai IFC. The inner operating system of most financial institution usually consists of complex network of either laws or regulations. What's more, this system relies on the stability of financial market in which they operate. Culturing a global finance center requires getting a delicate balance between excessive regulation that makes it too "expensive" to operate and too light a level of regulation that leaves public investors exposed to financial instability. Excessively light regulation is even more harmful if it is visible to outside parties, since they may worry about the potential repercussions on them from any problems that follow.

The development of infrastructure

As Shanghai continues to improve its infrastructure condition to realize its IFC blueprint by 2020, the city focuses on developing three major financial markets of bonds, equities and derivatives.

Since 2005, China's bond market has experienced significant development with the introduction of market-oriented products. In September 2010, the China Banking Regulatory Commission, the China Securities Regulatory Commission, and the People's Bank of China issued a notice to further develop Shanghai's bond exchange market by encouraging commercial banks to reenter after a 15-year market ban issued by the State Council before.

In China's derivatives market, several products were launched in 2010, including Shanghai-Shenzhen Equity Index Futures and RMB interest Rate swap, which began trading in January 2011. Going forward, the Shanghai Futures Exchange reportedly is planning to accept foreign traders' participation in direct commodity trading to expand the exchange market over the next five years.

Meanwhile, Shanghai's equities market keeps promoting openness to foreign investors with efforts to introduce more quality foreign institutional investors (QFII). Recently, it has accelerate the increase of RMB QFII (namely RQFII), as fresh long-term value for investors to its immature market. Beyond this, Shanghai continues to offer tax and rental privilege to launch its regional headquarters or branch here, advancing the city's goal to be an IFC.

The shortage of infrastructure

Chinese law and regulation have been quite conservative about what financial products are allowed in the market. Many of the more sophisticated products, especially in the derivatives area, are not allowed in China. Even some of the basic products are only partially available. This makes it harder to unleash Shanghai's potential to dominate Chinese derivatives transactions by building on its commodities exchange, for example. It may be that conservative regulation remains appropriate, but it does have the effect of limiting potential market growth.

It is difficult to overstate the importance of this issue. Global finance centers thrive on their ability to provide a full range of sophisticated products and services. Being very good at half or three-quarters of an overall task is not good enough, since it is relatively easy to choose London or New York instead, locations where everything can be done efficiently.

Shanghai's municipal government is clearly very aware of the need to expand the range of financial products and institutions in the city in order to be a truly global financial center. However, forward progress will depend on decisions by the central government of China, since Shanghai's municipal government has no authority to make decisions on these issues. China appears to be moving in the direction necessary for Shanghai's development, but at a quite measured pace, which may leave Shanghai at a major disadvantage for years.

Existing problems in the regulation

One particularly challenging area is the complex regulatory structure in China's financial market. Plenty of companies devote lots of time and money to deal with several separated regulatory agencies. Let's take the OTC equity market as an example. At the national level, China Security Regulatory Commission and China's Securities Association are responsible for watching almost each proceeding in public stock trade from IPO, reissue, dividends, distribution, delisting, you name it, which seriously harms the market's self-innovation and independence. Also the complex respective regional branch networks existing in China's every authority level bring about big inefficiencies to this system. However, the overhaul of market inefficiency produces riskless market environment to some extent.

This leads to an ambiguous phenomenon that regulatory execution heavily depends on the local administrators. Given that regional governments implement various policies, it is difficult for companies to follow a standardized rule or measure when they engage in cross-regional business. Moreover, a decentralized power structure in regulating finance system causes conflicts of interest, insider trading, and vicious competition among local municipalities.

Expected reform in regulation

To successfully develop Shanghai into an IFC, removing various financial regulatory roadblocks will need to be addressed at the national level. China should develop transparent, unambiguous regulations governing all sectors of financial market and establish specific role divisions within regulatory bodies. China also should ensure equal treatment in terms of capital requirements and distribution permission for foreign banking financial institutions.

In China's bond markets, for example, a complicated regulatory system makes the approval process for issuing corporate bonds difficult and time consuming. A unified regulatory body and transparent approval system are important to introduce higher foreign engagement.

Meanwhile, in the derivatives market, China should simplify the regulatory structure to avoid inconsistency of multiple regulatory bodies in terms of licensing, approval procedure and market restriction. Specific role divisions should be established among various regulators to ensure a coordinated regulatory approach to market activities.

4 Future Orientation of Shanghai IFC

4.1 Shanghai's ambitious goal

The official plan for Shanghai IFC

The Chinese government announced an ambitious blueprint in

February 2009 to build Shanghai into an international finance center by 2020.

This plan calls for Shanghai to build a mature financial system, boosting well-established financial institutions, advanced markets and a wide range of globally competitive financial products and services.

Is this plan for Shanghai achievable?

As China's financial, industrial and commercial center, Shanghai offers a compelling environment to establish an IFC. So far, the city has made excellent progress towards building necessary foundations to achieve its goal.

Shanghai boasts the world's 4th largest stock exchange in terms of trading value and the 6th largest market capitalization. Around half of all foreign financial institutions in China, including local headquarters of 21 foreign commercial banks are located here. In addition, Shanghai has China's largest commodity exchange as well as the unique financial future exchange. The trading value of its debt market is the second largest in Asia, just behind Japan.

By glimpsing Table 4-1, we can figure out Shanghai is undertaking a vital role as the pioneer of China's economy openness. Additionally, the robust support and beneficial guidance put forward by the government, especially after the official acknowledgement announced by China central government recently, will further promote Shanghai's boom.

Table 4-1 Institutions and their Statuses in Shanghai

Institutions	Status
Foreign exchange trading center	Head office at national level
Shanghai Gold Exchange	The only in China
Note market service center	Principal one in China
Shanghai petroleum market	The unique in mainland
China financial futures exchange	The only derivative market in China

Source: Young et al. (eds.) (2009: 234)

In 2010, Shanghai's financial markets facilitated an overall trading volume of RMB386.2 trillion, roughly 10 times the amount recorded 5 years earlier. A January 2012 plan jointly released by National Development and Reform Commission (NDRC) and Shanghai Municipal Government called for that number to reach RMB 1,000 trillion by 2015. On the other hand, the city continues to attract a substantial amount of worldwide top financial institutions, as the aggregated number reaches to 1,136 at the end of 2011.

4.2 Suggestions

Shanghai's plan to become an IFC is well under way, nonetheless, a great deal of work remaines to be done without much time left before the 2020 deadline.

In this part, let's concentrate on those problems mentioned before and propose our suggestions on 3 main issues substantially undermining Shanghai's competitiveness:

Implementing Market-oriented interest rate

Shanghai is heading down the path of formatting the market-oriented interest rate, but there are still a number of things that need to be done between central authority and municipal Shanghai government.

To tackle the problem of a market-oriented interest rate, it's suggested that Shanghai start with reducing government interference. In fact, in China today the government still assumes an important role in the financial sector. For instance, in the case of indirect finance, government investment is the most important driving force for China's economy, the main source of bank deposit and largest loan issuer. IPOs and reissuing of shares are seriously controlled by the China Securities Regulatory Commission, which brings about lots of problems, such as bribery, moral problems, conflict of interest between issuers and public investors. Therefore, China's policymakers have to change the prevailing pattern that government's intervention and initiatives take precedent over market mechanisms in order to promote Shanghai to an IFC.

In addition, stepping up efforts to liberalize China's capital market will also be of great help to this problem. We suppose the most important step is to allow free convertibility of the RMB against other currencies. What empirical lessons we learn from the mature IFCs are to never launch free mechanisms of cross-border capital flows too late. Another necessary step that China should follow is to release the existing market regulatory mechanisms to be more elastic, such as further broadening the approval of Qualified Foreign Institutional Investor (QFII) and Qualified Domestic Institutional Investor (QDII). This would complete the investment platform for both foreign and native investors to diversify their asset allocation in either overseas or domestic markets. Undoubtedly, both the further financial reforms and reduction of government intervention also are important elements for Shanghai to become an IFC with a comparative advantage.

Completing infrastructure environment

The next point to be addressed is Shanghai's ongoing development in infrastructure, both on the physical infrastructure, intellectual capital for financial institutions and human capital.

With regard to diversification and risk management, only by innovating more financial products, particularly financial derivatives can we satisfy various investors' demands, e.g. bond futures, foreign exchange futures, stock options. This will create new profitability further incurring a strong predictable market booming in near future.

In addition, China's central government should also cooperate with Shanghai local officials in the field, such as improving efficiency and transparency in the city's legal and accounting system as well as introducing incentives to attract financial professionals. Furthermore, developing a credible market culture will benefit the infrastructure construction. Abiding by the market-oriented principle, we should introduce more financial intermediates to replace the original functions of some government agencies. We should further develop a credit evaluation system for capital market to promote trade transparency and creditableness.

Next by establishing and perfecting intellectual property rights (IPRs), China is supposed to create more innovation, and bring more dynamism into the financial sector.

Solutions to the problem of "human resource (HR)"
Lack of skilled human resources always haunts the Chinese financial industry, as mentioned in Part III.

The data referring to this issue can be found in the report *'How to Attract and Retain Talent* issued in early 2013. The paper points out that " personal growth " and " personal work-life balance" are the top two factors driving job decisions for workers in financial industry rather than material incentives as most people considered. Career development and exploiting the potential of their own talents have come to be the most critical factors influencing employees.

Another good suggestion provided by Prof. Yang Mu and Lim Tin Seng is that some of the new roles that Hong Kong could assume, considering the Shanghai aspiration, may include an education hub to train Mainland Chinese to become qualified financial and business professionals. Through this mechanism, a "win-win" outcome can be expected.

Considering these factors cited before, Shanghai plans to improve the city's living environment, including developing advanced medical, cultural, and educational services, as well as subsidizing the education of foreign professionals' children and providing other incentives to attract and retain highly qualified foreign professionals. With the endeavor of perfecting the social welfare system, Shanghai is working hard to build a talent base that can drive the city to be a competitive IFC and shipping hub.

5 Conclusions

In this paper, we conclude that Shanghai is endowed with superior geographical conditions and relatively advantaged macroeconomic conditions. Shanghai benefits from the rise of China, and is considered as a promising IFC in the next few years. However, comparing with other advanced IFCs such as London and Hong Kong, Shanghai still has much to do.

The main results of our research are that, although aiming to be an IFC Shanghai is still weak in attracting high-qualified talent in the financial industry, and it lags far behind other IFCs in infrastructure construction. However, some effective measures have been already taken by authorities, which is a positive sign for the prospects of Shanghai IFC construction.

Considering the problems mentioned above, some practical suggestions are given, such as implementing market-oriented interest rates, completing the infrastructure environment, as well as some feasible solutions to the problem of human capital, e.g. cooperating with Hong Kong in the financial education field, improving Shanghai's living environment and upgrading social welfare system.

Shanghai today stands as the dominant financial center of China and is gradually realizing its ambition of re-emerging as the leading IFC of the world. In the near future, the gorgeous blueprint of Shanghai IFC is waiting for us to devote our all creativity and passions to make it come true.

References

Yang M., and Sang, L.T. (2010). Why China Needs to Build Shanghai into an IFC. *International Journal of China Studies*, pp. 125-140.

Ralph L. (2012). Shanghai as an IFC—Aspiration, Reality, Implication, *Undergraduate Economic Review*, (8)1, Article 14.

Scott T. (2009). Shanghai: Global Finance Center? Aspirations and Reality, and Implications for Hong Kong. Available at http: //www.hkjournal.org/PDF/2009_winter/3.pdf.

Douglas J. E. (2011). Building a Global Finance Center in Shanghai, Observations from Other centers. *China center at Brookings,* 1-19.

The American Chamber of Commerce in Shanghai. (2012). *Shanghai*, White Paper,

321-330.

The American Chamber of Commerce in Shanghai. (2012). *An Assessment of Shanghai's plan to become an International Finance Center by 2020.* pp.36-56.

Xiao, J. (2009). School of Finance, Shanghai vs. Hong Kong from the perspective of IFC construction. *Shanghai Institute of Foreign Trade*, 1-24.

Ben, D. (2013). Kelly Global Workforce Index, How to Attract and Retain Talent — An Industry Perspective on Financial Services, *global solutions manager for Kelly service*, 1-12.

Chapter 4

Shanghai International Financial Center

Hsin-Jen Wen[1], Hsiao-Ting Huang[2], Bei-Yu Gao[3],
Tzu-Han Kao [4]
Takming University of Science and Technology Team
Coach: Calvin S. Weng[*]

1 The Purpose of Project

The international financial crisis has accelerated the adjustment of the economic and financial situation of the world. In recent years, the position of emerging market and developing countries has gradually increased in the global economy. Especially countries like China, India and other Asian countries were the first to recover from the financial crisis and to further promote the economic situation of Asia toward global status (Radelet and Sachs, 1998). The rapid economic development and the growing economic strength of Asia continually

---

[1] Hsin-Jen Wen is an undergraduate majoring in Banking and Finance at Takming University of Science and Technology.
[2] Hsiao-Ting Huang is an undergraduate majoring in International Trade at Takming University of Science and Technology.
[3] Bei-Yu Gao is an undergraduate majoring in International Trade at Takming University of Science and Technology.
[4] Tzu-Han Kao is an undergraduate majoring in Applied Foreign Language at Takming University of Science and Technology.
[*] Calvin S. Weng is an Associate Professor in the Department of Banking and Finance at Takming University of Science and Technology. He received his doctorate of statistics and actuarial science from Roosevelt University (Chicago).

made the global multinational financial institutions tilt toward the Asian region, and further the possibility of creating a global financial center like New York or London in Asia (Gaubatz, 2005).

Over the past four decades, Taiwan has committed to economic development and created a considerable achievement (Siew, 1994). These efforts not only greatly enhanced the international status of Taiwan, but also maintained the stability of the exchange rate in Asian financial crisis. This outstanding performance won the high praise from foreign media, and Taiwan further become a solid cornerstone of finance in Asia-Pacific (Ma, 1994). Looking back at its economic development process, the Taiwan government has strategically developed the national economy by internationalization, liberalization, orderly sequence, and further overcame the various inherent limitations of economic conditions (Schive, 1994). This experience can provide Shanghai a reference to establish an international financial center.

In the 21st century, there are no boundaries for the global economy. Shanghai is facing some domestic and international challenges from other countries. First, the internal economic structure: traditional industries were gradually replaced by new technology and professional services industries. A variety of economic problems have become more complicated (Karreman and van der Knaap, 2007). Second, the external environment: the trend of economic liberalization has brought a new situation to the global economy, affecting the long-term economic development of Shanghai as well. Due to the competition from domestic and the significant change of foreign economic conditions, Shanghai needs to develop new competitive strategies. Building Shanghai as an "international financial center" is the right thing to do (Laurencon and Kam, 2005). The goal of Shanghai as an international financial center is to enhance the competitiveness of Shanghai and give Shanghai international standing in the 21st century. The purpose of this project is to transfer the past valuable experience of Taiwan. Liberalization, internationalization and high efficiency are the core concepts to create a good investment environment, and also create a superior living environment for Shanghai. Furthermore, it will allow Shanghai a foremost position in Asia.

2 The Advantages of the Financial Center

In 2009, the total amount of economic output of China was third in the world. The total amount of exports was number one in the world. The total amount of imports was the second in the world. In 2010, the Chinese economiy was estimated to be the second economy in the world (Ministry of Commerce, 2007); Therefore, Shanghai needs to become an international financial center to provide the corresponding financial service. And Shanghai has many advantages.

The goal of constructing Shanghai as an international financial center is to promote the economic liberalism in Shanghai and a high degree of internationalization (Sung, 2009). Let goods, funds and information and services conveniently circulate. The advantages of Shanghai are as follows.

First; Shanghai is the main financial market in China including the stock market (Shanghai Stock Exchange), the commodity futures market (Shanghai Futures Exchange), the foreign exchange market, short-term money market funds and bonds lending market (China Foreign Exchange Trading Center), financial futures markets (China Financial Futures Exchange), the gold market (Shanghai Gold Exchange) and so on. At present, Shanghai basically has formed the nationwide money market system including the stock, the bond, the currency, the foreign exchange, the gold, commodity futures. Shanghai plas many financial markets.

Second; along with the expansion of economic scale and the open policy of financial reformation, the money market scale of Shanghai is rapidly expand, and market function is obviously promoted.

Third; in recent years, the international position of financial market of Shanghai is steadily promoted. In 2009, the trade volume of Shanghai stock market was ranked third in the world.

Shanghai is located in Southeast Asia with economic potential, complet trade network, solid industry foundation and capability of development. All of these give Shanghai the opportunity to stand on the world stage in the 21st century.

In order to fully utilize the conditions of Shanghai to make Shanghai an international financial center, this plan suggests Shanghai should establish six centers as follows.

3 The Establishment of Shanghai International Financial Center

In order to make Shanghai become an international financial center, the establishment of six centers enhances Shanghai's degree of liberalization and internationalization (Schive, 1994; Schenk, 2002; Zhao, 2003).

3.1 Manufacturing Center

Developing the manufacturing center is to encourage enterprises by using Shanghai as a central location for the East Asia division of the production of high value-added product and marketing. The purpose of this center is to further enhance research and development capabilities, strengthen the continent's manufacturing base, and expand the long-term sustainability of the economic niche, while accelerating the development of high-tech industry. This is to build Shanghai as a High-Tech Island.

In order to achieve this goal, the Shanghai government should improve industrial environment, promote the ability of research and development of industries.

In addition, Shanghai should also develop strategic alliances of nation-wide enterprises to help international corporations to establish operation centers in Shanghai.

3.2 Shipping Center

Developing a shipping center is to let Shanghai become the location of container re-exports in East Asia and related additional value activity

(Sung, 2009). The purpose of this center is to circulate the goods in East Asia and strengthen the business function of Shanghai in the Asia-Pacific region.

Shanghai is a trade-based economy. The total amount of import and export have a significantl impact on Shanghai. Therefore, developing the shipping transportation center can circulate the goods of Shanghai and the East Asia region, and reform Shanghai to become the Pacific Asia operation center. Furthermore, it can support Shanghai to develop into a medium high-tech into a manufacturing center.

Moreover, in order to shorten the average clearance time, Shanghai should effectively establish an on-line automation system of customs and an inspection-free clearance procedure for international shipping.

3.3 Air Transport Center

The idea is to develop Shanghai into a freight transportation center for all passengers in East Asia (Zhao, 2003). The purpose of this center is to build up and enlarge the network of personnel and the goods of conveyance between East Asia and North America. At the same time, the construction of an air transport center will also expand airport development of the region.

Shanghai develops air transport center to grasp the global air transport niche, to further circulate the import and export of people and goods and to enhance the incentives of multinational operations in Shanghai.

In addition to the transport of goods in Shanghai, the establishments of Shanghai international financial center needs to match with the sightseeing services for attracting travelers.

The establishment of air transport center is based on the Pudong International Airport. The center can promote the development of the neighborhood around the center through land development planning.

3.4 Core Financial Center

Shanghai is engaged in the development of transnational financial services to serve the country and global Finances (Karreman, and van der Knaap, 2007). The purpose of this center is to grasp the global financial situation and build up high-efficiency, large-scale financial divisions in Shanghai.

Along openning the financial market of mainland China and the international financial markets, Shanghai has the huge propensity to develop the management of properties and assets.

In order to become an influent international financial center, Shanghai has to advance its currency and make the RMB an international currency. The development of an nternational financial center makes Shanghai progress more rapid, RMB internationalization will also push development forward more quickly.

3.5 Telecommunication Center

The development of Shanghai as a telecommunication center provides regional telecommunication service. In order to help local and foreign enterprises in Shanghai, the purpose of this center is to provide reasonable prices, high quality telecommunication service, and to establish a regional communication network. On the other hand, Shanghai can grasp the opportunity of a global telecommunication market and establish the world-class telecommunications.

Especially, the promotion of manufacturing center, shipping center, air transport center, core financial center and media center must rely on the support of telecommunication. In order to develop a higher level industry especially in service and the financial industry, Shanghai needs a strong telecommunication infrastructure. If there are no flourishing and cheap communication facilities, the transnational corporation will not take Shanghai into account for consideration of a headquarters.

3.6 Media Center

The development of the media center is to adjust to the trend of the integration of international media business. To spread out the business scope, the development combines satellite television and the local area of cable T.V. in Shanghai. The purpose of this center is to help Shanghai control the media market of the region, make life convenient and business information available. At the same time, Shanghai may develop diverse cultures for attracting people and enabling them to enjoy life.

Satellite television and cable T.V. can become the main tool for delivery of international information in the 21st century. If Shanghai can make use of the advantage of language and culture to provide good quality service and to attract the domestic and international operator to invest, Shanghai will become the supply center of global Chinese programming, like Hong Kong or Singapore.

4 Summary

The keys to a Shanghai international financial center are "liberalization" and "internationalization" as follows. First, to circulate the goods, services, people and capital. Second, to facilitate the flow of information and remove unnecessary regulation of economic activity or untimely provision. Third, let foreigners in Shanghai enjoy the same treatment as nationals (Gaubatz, 2005; Jao, 2003).

Simply speaking, the specific idea for developing Shanghai as an international financial center is to create a high degree of liberalization and internationalization of the overall economic environment in which the goods, services, people, capital and information can conveniently be accessed and circulated. The Shanghai international financial center is to attract multinational corporations and local enterprises to invest or operate in Shanghai.

References

Gaubatz, P. (2005). *Globalization and the Development of New Central Business Districts in Beijing, Shanghai and Guangzhou*, In Laurence J. C. Ma and Fulong Wu

(Ed.), Restructuring the Chinese city: Changing Society, Economy and Space. London, New York: Routledge, chapter 6, pp. 98-121.

Karreman, B., and van der Knaap, B. (2007). *The Financial Centres of Shanghai and Hong Kong: Competition or Complementarity?* Erim Report Series Research in Management.

Laurencon, J. and Kam K. T. (2005). Shanghai's Development as an International Financial Center. *Review of Pacific Basin Financial Markets and Policies*, 8(1), 147-66.

Ministry of Commerce (MC), PRC editor. 2007. Report on Foreign Investment in China 2007. Beijing: Ministry of Commerce.

Sung, Y. W. (2009). *Hong Kong and Shanghai as Global Service Hubs: Rivalry or Complementarity?* Occasional Paper No. 20, Shanghai-Hong Kong Development Institute, The Chinese University of Hong Kong.

Radelet, S. and Sachs, G. (1998). The East Asian Financial Crisis: Diagnosis, Remedies and Prospects. *Brookings Papers on Economic Activity*, 1, 1-90.

Schive, C. (1994). Regional Operations Center and the ROC Economy in the 1990s. *Industry of Free China* April, 43-53.

Siew, V. C. (1994). The Changing Role of Taiwan in East Asian Economic Grouping. *Industry of Free China* April, 23-27.

Ma, K. (1994). The Retrospect and Prospect of Taiwan's Economy. *Economic Outlook*, 9(1), 59-64.

Schenk, C. R. (2002). Banks and the Emergence of Hong Kong as an International Financial Center. *Journal of International Financial Markets, Institutions and Money*, 12 (4-5), 321-40.

Zhao, S. X. B. (2003). Spatial Restructuring of Financial Centers in Mainland China and Hong Kong: A Geography of Finance Perspective. *Urban Affairs Review*, 38(4), 535-71.

Gaubatz, P. (2005). Globalization and the Development of New Central Business Districts in Beijing, Shanghai and Guangzhou, In Laurence J. C. Ma and Fulong Wu (Ed.), Restructuring the Chinese city: changing society, economy and space. London, New York: Routledge, chapter 6, pp. 98-121.

Jao, Y. C. (2003). *Shanghai and Hong Kong as International Financial Centres: Historical Perspective and Contemporary Analysis.* Working paper No. 1071, Hong Kong Institute of Economics and Business Strategy, The University of Hong Kong.

Chapter 5

Shanghai Finance Center and Africa's Experiences

Doreen Kifumani[1], Saunath Tayah[2], Jonathan Muromba[3]
African Union Team
Coach: Wenguo Liu[*]

1 What Is a Financial Center?

Before we examine what makes financial centers successful, we should define them. The definition of a financial center is bound up in the definition of a city. We can start by observing that financial centers are cities or districts of cities where finance is conducted. However, the definition of a city is problematic, as anyone who has tried to compare city populations knows. Is Paris bigger than London? Did you mean the core city, perhaps the medieval walls, the city as defined by political boundaries, the greater metropolitan area? In certain cases, such as offshore centers like the Cayman Islands, the financial center is really just the jurisdiction.

---

[1] Doreen Kifumani comes from Tanzania, she is an undergraduate majoring in International Trade and Economics at Shanghai Finance University.
[2] Saunath Tayah comes from Tanzania, she is an undergraduate majoring in International Trade and Economics at Shanghai Finance University.
[3] Jonathan Muromba comes from Zimbabwe, he is an undergraduate majoring in International Trade and Economics at Shanghai Finance University.
[*] Wenguo Liu is a full time professor in School of Accounting at Shanghai Finance University. His research focuses on accounting, entrepreneurial finance.

Likewise, the definition of finance is problematic. All cities have financial transactions. Is the shipping transaction finance? Paying for fuel? When does a shipping transaction become just finance? Are we talking about transactions that are wholly financial? Funding a vessel, insuring it? So much finance is conducted electronically that one might be able to claim that server farms located anywhere are financial centers.

Interestingly, the OECD doesn't define financial centers yet it defines offshore financial centers starting with, "Countries or jurisdictions with financial centers that contain financial institutions. While the omission of normal financial centers from the OECD glossary strikes us as a large oversight, I do think they point us at the heart of the issue, so my definition might be "financial centers are places with strong concentrations of financial professionals and their firms". It's the people that matter.

Most papers and financial sites define them as follows:

A financial center is a global city that is home to a large number of internationally significant banks, businesses, and stock exchanges.

An international financial center is a non-specific term usually used to describe an important participant in international financial market trading. An international financial center (sometimes abbreviated to *IFC*) will usually have at least one major stock market.

Different ranking system like the Global Financial Centre Index is compiled by the London-based British think-tank Z/Yen and is published annually by the City of London Corporation, the Xinhua News Agency of China, partnering with the Chicago Mercantile Exchange and Dow Jones & Company of the United States and the Atlantic and its senior-editor Richard Florida. They all presented different ranking observing Shanghai does not fall in any top 5 ranking.

2 Why Do We Study Financial Centers?

Financial centers funnel investment toward innovation and growth. Vibrant, competitive financial centers give cities economic advantages in information, knowledge and access to capital. A strong financial center, whether domestic, niche, regional, international or global, connects the wider economy to the global financial community. Cities that are part of the global financial network chain form global trade and growth. Inward and outward investment opportunities increase the wealth of cities that have financial centers and the wealth of their citizens.

'Traffic' between the domestic economy and the global financial community is critical to national economic performance. The key function of the domestic financial community is not its ability to service the domestic economy's needs domestically, rather its ability to service the domestic economy's needs wherever and however they are best serviced. But after a point a well functioning financial center attracts global financial transactions in its own right, and this confuses matters.

2.1 Financial center roles

Successful financial centers can and do fulfill more than one role:
- "Global" financial centers that are truly global focused, where only a few can claim that role, London, New York, Hong Kong and Singapore;
- "International" financial centers such as Seoul or Shanghai or Frankfurt that conduct a significant volume of cross-border transactions;
- "Niche" financial centers that are worldwide leaders in one sector, such as Hamilton in reinsurance or Zurich and Edinburgh in fund management;
- "National" financial centers, often within federal countries, that act as the main financial center for financial services within one country, such as Toronto or Frankfurt;
- "Regional" financial centers that conduct a large proportion of regional business within one country, e.g. Boston or Vancouver.

2.2 Evolution of a financial center

There are five key areas of financial center competitiveness:

- "People" — the availability of good personnel and the flexibility of the labor markets;
- "Business Environment" — regulation, tax rates, levels of corruption and ease of doing business;
- "Market Access" — levels of trading, as well as clustering effects from having many financial service firms together in one center;
- "Infrastructure" — the cost and availability of property and transport links;
- "General Competitiveness" — the concept that the whole is "greater than the sum of the parts".

2.3 Win-win financial centers?

The role of cooperation amongst financial centers is another area worthy of much more study. Although financial centers compete with one another, the competition is not a "zero-sum" game.

How can financial center competition be win-win?

In theory, wider global allocation of risk and reward increases overall economic efficiency. In practice, the ability to tap cheaper capital for inward investment increases overall economic activity for the host country, increases portfolio diversification for the investor, and thus benefits both. More prosaically, a back office in Mumbai supporting a Singapore trading operation benefits both financial centers.

More deals mean a bigger pie for everybody. Business people are attracted to jurisdictions with fair and stable rules (we often wonder if that's why business people use so many sports metaphors — a firm belief that somebody enforces stable rules fairly seems core to their being). Business people like governments without too much party fanaticism, because party fanaticism means the rules of the game can be changed rapidly. Business people can handle uncertainty. A fair and stable system is not necessarily predictable, but system rules should be stable and rule changes predictable, which almost certainly implies numerous stakeholders and a wide policy. So an "open" business center is important. This may be of increasing significance as governments, now the shamed owners of concentrated banks, may be tempted to rewrite rules to favor domestic players.

An open competitive environment helps to encourage diversity. The resulting open and diverse financial center ecosystem can be very robust. Still, this doesn't explain how moving jobs from London to Singapore helps London. A financial center has a high fixed infrastructure — expensive ICT, buildings, transport, accommodation, schools. The primary measure of success cannot just be financial center jobs. The measure for financial centers should be how effective they are at providing choice and access to global financial services. Then domestic and global markets both win. On this measure, protected domestic financial players are clearly a hindrance. Global finance is a non-zero sum game, but only for those centers who accept that they have to be open and diverse. Open competition leads to appropriate connectivity with the global financial markets.

3 What Are the Global Financial Centers Today?

London and New York are clearly the leading financial centers in the world today and the only two that most observers would define as truly global financial centers. It appeared in the 1980's that Tokyo would eventually also obtain this status, but the bursting of the Japanese financial and real estate bubbles, and the ensuing "lost decade," seem to have eliminated that momentum. There are also powerful forces of institutional inertia holding Tokyo back, as discussed later.

Similarly, it appeared for a time that Germany would achieve its national ambition of establishing "Finanzplatz Deutschland", effectively meaning that Frankfurt would join the ranks of global financial centers on the back of its role as the economic center of a rising Europe. However, London to a lesser extent, New York responded effectively to the German challenge and much of the European business that Frankfurt hoped to capture instead flowed to London or became global rather than simply European, with a piece going to New York.

Hong Kong is sometimes seen as a truly global financial center, such as in the analysis accompanying the most recent GFCI surveys.

However, many other observers still see a significant gap between it and the duo of London and New York. Also, there is a concern that Hong Kong is so reliant on Chinese business that it may fall in relative terms as more of this business is conducted through Shanghai and perhaps other mainland Chinese financial centers.

3.1 London as a global financial center

London — treating all comers fairly

The heritage of London and the UK is treating all comers fairly — the so-called Wimbledon effect — the local champion may have little chance, but the judging will be fair. London thrives when it's open to foreigners, from French Huguenots to Hong Kong Chinese. London suffers when it's unfair to foreigners — the expulsion of the Jews in 1290 or the closed shops of brokers and jobbers until 1986.

London has been built on others' mistakes. Eurodollar markets grew swiftly in the 1960s when US tax rule changes meant multinationals found it attractive to leave dollars outside the control of US authorities. Then in the 1980s, US companies began to borrow offshore, finding Euro markets an advantageous place for holding excess liquidity, providing short-term loans and financing imports and exports. Sarbanes-Oxley requirements after 2000 increased the attractiveness of London as a "light touch" regulatory environment. AIM listings increased listings at the expense of NYSE. It's a good discussion point as to whether US litigation itself prevents principles-based regulation in the US. But when the UK makes mistakes, for example with the shipping industry last year, retribution is non-existent, but exodus is swift.

What are London's overall strengths and weaknesses?

London probably has the broadest and deepest presence as a truly global financial center that is, counting only transactions that do not have a native English element to them but which are structured and executed in London because of the strength of its people and institutions. There are experts in virtually every conceivable type of financial transaction and sub-sector of finance in London and the specialized legal and other experts to support them.

English law is clear and well-understood and the courts and regulators are viewed as being generally predictable and fair.

Further, the financial business is such an important part of the UK economy and its trade balance that governments of all political parties have generally tried to promote London's status as a financial center. (This has been less true in the immediate wake of the financial crisis but even now, the government is leery of taking steps that might permanently impair London's position in these markets.)

London has high quality financial professionals and support services, many of them coming from other parts of Europe or from the US, lured both by the career opportunities and by the excellent quality of life available in that vibrant city.

Virtually everyone agrees that London will remain a global financial center due to its very strong position today and its long history as a leader.

However, the city has weaknesses as well as strengths. It is a high cost city, both in terms of business costs and the costs of living for its professionals. Real estate is particularly expensive, partly because the traditional financial district is quite constricted geographically and subject to many building restrictions to preserve its historical character.

This pressure has been partly relieved by the growth of the Canary Wharf financial district, but that has the disadvantage of being some distance from the cultural and other attractions of London. The congestion has also meant increasingly bad commuting times, made worse by infrastructure problems with the main rail lines, including the aging Underground.

Crime has also become an increasing problem in terms of recruitment in London, especially as crime rates in its business, and the people and institutions it supports, based purely on the American business. This would make it easier to overcome temporary bumps in the road.

The more domestic focus in New York does have the potential disadvantage that it could lead to greater insularity and a loss of the "edge" that is necessary to compete in global markets. However, history has shown that the US investment banks have expanded to become very strong competitors in Europe while European players have not had quite the same level of success in coming to the US and Asian firms play a fairly limited role in the US market.

In addition, New York has generally been rated as more innovative than London, even in recent surveys, although Londoners protest loudly at this characterization. There may also be a reassessment over time of that innovation, if the view of some observers gains wider acceptance, that much of the financial innovation in the US was actually harmful.

3.2 What are New York City's overall strengths and Weaknesses?

New York's story is quite similar to London's in that it is the other great world financial center and has been for many years. Thus, it also has a wide and deep set of markets, personnel, and institutions that give it a strong position for the future.

Differences between New York and London

One of the differences is that New York is somewhat less global than London, in that a substantial portion of the business has a natural American connection, with one or both sides of the transaction are based in the US. This is a great strength of New York, since its vast hinterland in the US means that even if its global competitiveness temporarily slips, it will be able to maintain a very large volume of financial center business.

Tokyo was the major business city in Asia and was at the heart of the second-largest economy in the world. That economy had succeeded remarkably in the preceding decades, helping to propel its financial markets to record highs in terms of price levels and volumes of activity. As a result, foreign investment and commercial banks generally put their Asian headquarters in Tokyo or, at the least, established a major presence in Tokyo.

Yet, today, several decades later, Tokyo is not truly a global financial center and there are relatively few who believe it will become one soon. What stopped it?

Clearly, the bursting of its major bubbles in real estate and equity markets, followed by well over a decade of anemic overall growth in the economy, were major factors.

However, there are a number of institutional and policy factors that contributed mightily to the failure, which Shanghai would be well-advised to avoid.

First, regulatory and political decisions, and the resulting institutional structures and operations, were very largely designed with an inward-looking view. Perhaps its rapid success, pulled off in its own unique way and not in straight forward limitation of Western development, contributed to a tendency to find "Japanese" solutions that were highly tailored to domestic requirements and perceptions.

In addition, there were close ties between the Japanese financial firms and the larger business community, through the "keiretsu" structure of quasi-conglomerates and also through other means. The business community in turn had close ties to the long-ruling Liberal Democratic Party and the powerful bureaucracy and tended to use these ties to protect the status quo and to make it more difficult for outsiders, including foreigners, to compete.

Second, and partly as a result of the first point, Japan tended to regulate finance in a way that stifled new products and ways of doing business. New techniques that were developed in London or New York generally took many years to work their way into use in Japan. (It is telling, for example, that Singapore began trading futures on the Nikkei 225 stock index two years before Japan did.) This made it difficult to lure foreign business to Japan, since there were often more effective transaction structures available in other financial centers.

4 What Are the Key Lessons for Shanghai from All These Comparisons?

Shanghai starts with major advantages that give it a strong shot at developing into a truly global financial center. Even if it were to fail to meet this lofty goal anytime soon, (and there are many major world cities that have aspired to this role without success), it is a virtual certainty that Shanghai will become a major Asian regional financial center and perhaps the dominant one.

The city should work hard to ensure that it maintains its advantages and gains the maximum marketing benefit from them in terms of raising its desirability to global institutions and financial professionals.

On the other hand, there are clearly some genuine disadvantages, plus some perceived ones, on which the city should work. It should eliminate or counteract the true negatives and ensure that foreigners gain a better understanding of the actual situation in the case of excessively negative perceptions.

4.1 Gamoyo-Tanzania as an emerging East African financial center

Tanzania is located in the eastern part of Africa, bordering the Indian Ocean to its east. Tanzania is regarded as the East African hot spot due to its good harbor ports in Bagamoyo, Dar es Salaam, Tanga and Zanzibar.

Tanzania is a developing country, a member of the World Bank and IFM. Tanzania has had a great relationship with China since 1965. This year the China-Tanzania treaty was renewed officially in Tanzania-Bagamoyo when President Xi Jinping of China took a tour of Tanzania April 23, 2013.

Currently there 25 Chinese firms in Tanzania-Dar es salaam that brought a great benefits to Tanzania like more Job vacancies, diversity and growth in GDP.

4.2 A renewal of the China-Tanzania treaty of 1965

Back ground

Tanzania's strategic decision to promote stronger ties with China is entirely understandable but sometimes it makes the Western capitals nervous. Relations between Tanzania and China date back to the Cooperation Agreement signed 48 years ago. This treaty can be traced back to when the late President Nyerere visited China in 1965, when the Sino-Tanzanian Treaty of Friendship (1965) was signed in Peking on February 20, 1965. *This "Treaty of Friendship"* brought about a new era of cooperation between the People's Republic of China and the United Republic of Tanzania, and it was very instrumental in moving the new country forwards.

Tanzania's development can be clearly observed from the amount of financing extended to Tanzania in the early years after Independence. According to the report which was given to the national assembly in May 10, 1968, in a reply to the question about how much in loans Tanzania received since Independence, China was ranked second to Great Britain, where it extended a total of $40 million as of 31 December 1967. These loans were extended at the time which was most needed to equip the Tanzanian people with the skills and knowledge which transformed the country from a country with 85% of its adult population illiterate and a country with only two trained engineers and 12 doctors to a country which is going in the right direction in the fulfillment of bettering the life of its people.

Current affairs

In this modern era when China is projected to be the largest economy in the world by 2016, it is unnecessary to point out the great importance of Tanzania forging stronger ties with China; this is proven by the way in which all the great nations of the world are so eagerly competing to forge close ties with China and attract more FDI to their countries.

On the other hand, as China expands its presence in Africa, Beijing Geo-strategists understand the importance of Tanzania in implementing their foreign policy, such considerations underscore the fact that, Tanzania is well-positioned to advance Economic and trade cooperation between China and Africa. This can be observed with the current active role of China in Tanzania which signals the commitment of China investing in a long-term strategic partnership with Tanzania.

Equally important, while there is no doubt that this is a renewal of our friendship, it poses two important questions regarding the new era of Tanzania-China relations:

1. What kind of strategic relationship should Tanzania have with China?
2. What kind of strategic relationship can Tanzania have with China?

These are vital questions and we cannot turn blind eyes on them. Tanzania policymakers must be realistic about our role in the new China-Tanzania relation and we have to be realistic about our own strategic priorities and limitations.

We know the presence of mining, oil and Gas and other thriving extractive industries, this might sound silly, but let's be clear and let's be simple, strategy is about "choices", and at the root of all strategy lies the ability to make good choices. For that reason in a country where rural incomes are linked either directly or indirectly to agriculture, if we have to think strategically and if we want to give our people a fair share from the China-Tanzania relationship, then our choice should be Agriculture development for export to China and we shouldn't concentrate our energy in extractive Industries, which is a simple choice to take. Agricultural growth will make a direct contribution to the welfare of rural populations by raising the incomes of 80% of Tanzanian farmers and their families and that would be a very smart foreign policy choice.

Lastly, our good friendship with China should not go silent on the fact that; there may be an exceptional case where some Industry in Tanzania should be entitled to special protection from cheap China imports. Borrowing from Mwalimu Nyerere's speech when he visited China in 1968, he was noted, saying "The friendship between Tanzania and People's Republic of China is a friendship between most unequal equals". From that perspective, formulating a win to win trade policy in a relationship between unequal equals requires the ability to convey uncomfortable truth. Therefore while we are giving China open access to our market, we shouldn't be shy to highlight areas which we need to protect our local infant industries which is essential in improving the well being of our people and making us a more valuable partner in International Trade.

4.3 Projects under the China-Tanzania treaty

Tanzanian President Jakaya Kikwete and Chinese President Xi Jinping signed 16 agreements for development projects in mainland Tanzania and three agreements for Zanzibar during Xi's state visit to Dar es Salaam on March 24th-25th. The deal cleared the way for China to finance and build a 16-trillion shilling ($10 billion) port at Bagamoyo and other infrastructure projects.

"President Xi's visit is historic," Tanzania's Minister of Foreign Affairs and International Co-operation Bernard Membe told Sabahi. "Apart from unveiling China's policy towards Africa through Tanzania, Tanzania has signed with China 19 valuable agreements. An agreement like that of the port of Bagamoyo [project] is a lifelong investment."

Scheduled for completion by 2017, the port at Bagamoyo— northwest of Dar es Salaam — will be able to handle twenty times more cargo than the port in the Tanzanian capital, which is the country's largest port.

"The port [at Bagamoyo] will be of high standards. We are building a fourth generation port," said Tanzania's Ambassador to China. "It will handle 20 million containers a year, compared to [the port] of Dar es Salaam, which is handling only 800,000 containers a year."

The port construction project will include the building of a new 34-kilometre road joining Bagamoyo to Mlandizi and 65 kilometres of railway connecting Bagamoyo to the Tanzania-Zambia Railway (TAZARA) and Central Railway, Marmo told Sabahi.

The bilateral deals call for China to commit 800 billion Tanzanian shillings ($500 million) in 2013 for starting the port construction, he said.

The rest of the Chinese financial aid package will follow in 2014 and 2015, according to Membe.

Other projects under the Chinese-Tanzanian agreements include the creation of a modern agricultural and industrial zone, interest-free loans and loan agreements between the Export-Import Bank of China and the Bank of Tanzania, the establishment of a Chinese cultural center in Tanzania, the rehabilitation of the Abdullah Mzee Hospital in Zanzibar, and the provision of shipping container inspection equipment for the port of Zanzibar, the Tanzanian foreign minister said.

4.4 The benefits of the China-Tanzania treaty for China and Tanzania

The benefits of the China-Tanzania treaty to China and Tanzania are as follows: increase the level of investor's attraction, increases the market size; it stimulates economic diversity; it creates more Job opportunity due to new firms, it increases both the GDP and GNP level; in different projects it supports an increase in infrastructures like the bagamoyo-mlandizi railway line project; and generally, boosts the economic level in both countries.

4.5 The benefits of China-Tanzania treaty to the Shanghai finance center

The benefits of China-Tanzania treaty to the Shanghai finance center are as follows: it is an increase in a market size for china products; this will boost the firms and industries in China-Shanghai to increase its production level. It will attract more investors to china; an increase to the market size eventually will attract more investors to China-shanghai. The Shanghai Finance center will benefit fluent English expertise for Tanzania, hence lead to a push for its development.

The Chinese stand to gain from Tanzania's future port at Bagamoyo because it would facilitate China-bound shipments of minerals from Zambia, Zimbabwe and the Democratic Republic of Congo via the Indian Ocean, Marmo said.

The new port also would transform Bagamoyo into an East African hub for Indian Ocean shipments to and from six of Tanzania's mostly landlocked neighbors, ease congestion at the Dar es Salaam port and make Tanzania's import-export sector more efficient, said Vincent Nyerere, a parliamentarian and businessman.

Tanzania is losing a lot of trade and commerce because of inefficiency at the port of Dar es Salaam, Nyerere told Sabahi.

The neighboring countries of Malawi, Zambia, Democratic Republic of Congo, Burundi, Rwanda and Uganda would like to export and import products via Tanzania, the shortest and most viable route to the Indian Ocean, Nyerere said. But for now, these countries must do with the Kenyan port of Mombasa and the South African port of Durban, which are more distant and costly routes.

Kikwete thanked China for its decision to help Tanzania improve its infrastructure and provide access to interest-free or low-interest loans, as long as the bilateral relationship serves "the interests of Tanzania."

Key Measures to Support Shanghai's Development as a Financial Hub.

The Key Measures to Support Shanghai's Development as a Financial Hub are:

1. Conduct trade settlement in yuan on trial basis.

2. To fully tap the financial market in Shanghai in terms of clearing in yuan.

3. Develop over-the-counter markets for non-listed companies in the Yangtze River Delta.

4. Study a mechanism to help companies trade on the OTC markets to be transferred to the main stock boards.

5. Develop pension products that offer tax breaks to encourage people to pay into pensions.

6. Encourage more international development institutions to issue yuan denominated bonds.

7. Study plans to allow overseas enterprises to issue Yuan-denominated bonds in China.

8. To allow qualified overseas companies to issue yuan-denominated shares.

9. Step up the development of the re-insurance market.

10. Give priority in terms of business expansion to securities and fund management joint ventures.

11. Encourage financial institutions to cover a wider range of businesses.

12. Encourage the development of private equity and venture capital companies.

5 Shanghai Financial Center and Hong Kong Financial Center

5.1 Background

On Jul.26, 2012, One of Shanghai's vice mayors, Tu Guangshao, stated that "it would be preferable for Shanghai to be China's main financial center, and should be promoted over Hong Kong to capture global attention on China's markets." While Shanghai Communist Party chief Yu Zheng Sheng has conceded that Shanghai could not catch up with Hong Kong until 2020, the polarization of both cities as China's main financial center is an issue that still has a long way to go before being resolved.

Tu was the co-author of an influential report citing that Shanghai and not Hong Kong should be China's premier international financial center in the longer term, and recommended measures to make Shanghai a top international financial center by 2020, a policy adopted by the State Council in 2009.

"In the long run, it is impossible for China to have two international financial centers," said the report, which was issued by the Brookings-Tsinghua Center for Public Policy, the Beijing branch of the U.S.-based

Brookings Institution. "China will finally have only one financial center and that is Shanghai."

Several senior mainland officials co-authored the report, including the People's Bank of China governor Zhou Xiaochuan and Yi Gang, director of the State Administration of Foreign Exchange and deputy governor of the central bank. John Thornton, chairman of the Brookings Institution and a former Goldman Sachs Asia chief also contributed to the report, which recommended making the yuan fully convertible within a decade, a prerequisite that will enable Shanghai to be an offshore yuan center.

Not all authors were in agreement. Tu mentioned that in the eyes of the foreign observers, "Hong Kong is not like Shanghai, for it is only a regional market." Overall, in foreigners' eyes, Hong Kong is only part of China. Anyone having long-term strategic vision would say China's financial center will be in Shanghai. It represents how the world looks at China."

5.2 Which city should be the top dog for China?

The comparisons at times can be off-kilter, and Shanghai's politicians are long noted for their aggressiveness in making statements concerning Hong Kong. I recall previous vice mayors stating that by the time of the Beijing Olympics, Shanghai would already have overtaken Hong Kong as a financial center, however this has not happened. What then, are the differences between the two cities and what needs to be done to truly make Shanghai an international financial center to rival or even overtake its southern counterpart?

5.3 Shanghai as a financial center

It is important to recognize that Shanghai today is not an international financial center, although the city certainly likes to promote the fact that it is. There are a number of restrictions that apply to Shanghai that do not apply currently to the markets and status of Hong Kong. These include:

The RMB Yuan as an internationally tradable currency

Until China changes the current policy over the yuan and permits it to be a freely tradable currency, Shanghai cannot be an international financial center. The Hong Kong dollar is a tradable currency on the global currency markets. Consequently, currency trading is endemic in Hong Kong, and licensed money changers can be found on the streets. Mainland China maintains currency controls and until this is eased Shanghai will remain a yuan-denominated market only suitable for domestic China trade.

Mainland China stock markets are not open to foreign investors

Although the indexes in Shanghai are quoted internationally as a benchmark, in reality they are no such thing. Foreign investors are not permitted to purchase Mainland China stocks on the Shanghai or Shenzhen bourses, and in any event, the proportion of stock held by the government remains unfeasibly high to evade concerns over market fixing or vested interests. There is, in short, no direct link between the Shanghai market and any impact on stocks held in international jurisdictions. Why the Shanghai index continues to be regarded as influential when compared to internationally tradable markets in Hong Kong, Singapore and Tokyo continues to bemuse me.

A reform program is to be put into place to permit foreign companies to list, but this is rather different from allowing access to mainland stocks by foreign institutional investors. The Chinese government has a great need to get out of stocks it holds in its listed state-owned enterprises, and it needs to release the majority of these into public holdings. The problem is that in doing so, the massive amount of shares that would come onto the domestic market would seriously deflate prices. China is caught between managing stocks in companies it owns in a market it remains the regulator, and the alternative is being out of stocks and appointing an independent regulator. Neither of these two scenarios is under state consideration at the present.

Hong Kong's rule of law

Hong Kong still maintains a British-derived legal system, and has had a stock market since 1891. The market, Asia's second largest after Tokyo, has developed and retains a sound legal and regulatory system used to the dealings, disputes, claims and liabilities of international finance. Although Hong Kong does have a regulatory conflict between its commercial and regulatory position, generally speaking the market is well managed and possesses global credibility. Market manipulators, insider dealers and fraudsters are routinely jailed when caught, and the city retains an independent commission against corruption to monitor and look into such activities.

Mainland China is not in a position to provide that for Shanghai unless a massive evolution in the regulatory conflicts between state and commerce is undertaken. The past behavior also of some of China's own investment funds, including government-backed ones such as GITIC, and the constant play between China and Hong Kong over asset holdings and evasion of liabilities dictate that neither are able to fully appreciate the concepts of transparency and financial responsibility.

Hong Kong's role in Shanghai's ambition

The State Council's announcement to turn Shanghai into an international financial center by 2020 has raised concerns in Hong Kong. According to reports, Hong Kong is worried that Shanghai's ambition would undermine the city's position as an international financial center. To allay such fear, Shanghai's former Party Secretary Yu Zheng Sheng assured Hong Kong people that Shanghai is still lagging behind Hong Kong as a financial center in many aspects. Furthermore, it is also likely that Shanghai will continue to function as a regional financial center as the city continues to develop and liberalize its financial sector in the coming years. As one of the world's leading financial center, Hong Kong is also able to provide invaluable lessons for Shanghai to develop its financial sector, especially in areas such as liberalizing its capital market and improving its legal system. In addition, Hong Kong could also help Shanghai to improve the latter's corporate and commercial infrastructure.

Nonetheless, Hong Kong could overcome Shanghai's challenge and turn it into a "win-win" situation by revising its traditional role as the gateway to China for investors. Some of the new roles that it could adopt may include providing consulting services to Chinese businesses seeking to expand overseas or as an education hub to train Mainland Chinese to become qualified financial and business professionals. This process is not something new as the city has adapted before as it went from selling plastic flowers to higher levels of manufacturing before reaching the present state of being a global financial capital.

6 Conclusions

International financial centers are the places where all sorts of international financial services and legal services such as underwriting, trading, dealing and brokerage of services are produced, sold and exported. Shanghai with almost all kinds of financial markets established in the last twenty years has obvious potential to become China's international financial center.

However, there are two most important conditions: further financial reform (Shanghai really becomes the No. 1 financial center in China, but not Beijing) and the full convertibility of RMB are totally dependent on Beijing's leaders, but not marketable. There is no doubt that China's economy is going to exceed Japan's and US's, and RMB will be internationalized, and Shanghai will be China's international financial center, eventually. But, could it be completed in the next ten years? We need to watch it carefully.

From our point of view; Shanghai financial center will soon emerge as a world financial center, since it has many relationships with African countries like Tanzania, Zambia, Zimbabwe and many more which results in a very large market size, huge cash flow, brain drain leading to expertise, attracts more investors hence economic growth meaning a world successful financial center.

Also Shanghai, meaning the Chinese should observe the above conditions and good examples from London Financial center and New

York financial center as well as Hong Kong since it is a step ahead.

Finally, US students from the Shanghai Finance University have a good feeling that Shanghai will become the world financial center by 2020 since it has a good economic-financial foundation, strategies and policies guided under the People's Bank of China (PBC) and is a leading Asian financial center in the short-term meaning from now to 2015.

References

Alesina, A., Arnaud, D., William E., Sergio K. and Romain W. (2003). Fractionalization. *Journal of Economic Growth*, 8,155-194.

Alfaro, L., Sabnem K., and Vadym V. (2005). *Why Doesn't Capital Flow from Rich to Poor Countries? An Empirical Investigation*. NBER Working Paper, 11901.

Allen, F., Isaac O., and Lemma S. (2011). African Financial Systems: A Review. *Review of Development Finance*, 1, 79-113.

Allen, F., Elena C., Robert C., Jun Q., Lemma S., and Patricio V. (2011). *Improving Access to Banking: Evidence from Kenya*. Working paper, University of Pennsylvania.

Barth, J. R., Gerard C., and Ross L. (2001a). *The Regulation and Supervision of Banks around the World: A New Database*. Policy Research Working Paper 2588. World Bank.

Barth, J. R., Gerard C., and Ross L., (2001b). *Banking Systems around the Globe: Do Regulation and Ownership Affect Performance and Stability?* In Frederic S. M. (ed.), Prudential Regulation and Supervision: What Works and What Doesn't. University of Chicago Press, 31-96.

Chaia, A., Aparna D., Tony G., Maria J. G., Jonathan M., and Robert S. (2011). *Half the World is Unbanked*, New York University, working paper.

Claessens, S., Asli D. K., & Harry H. (2001). How Does Foreign Entry Affect Domestic Banking Markets? *Journal of Banking and Finance*, 25 (5), 891-911.

Claessens, S. and Luc L. (2003). What Drives Bank Competition? Some International Evidence, *Journal of Money*, Credit and Banking, 36(3), 563-583.

Detragiache, E., Thierry T., and Poonam G. (2006). *Foreign Banks in Poor Countries: Theory and Evidence*. IMF Working Paper, WP/06/18.

Easterly, W., & Ross L. (1997). Africa's Growth Tragedy: Policies and Ethnic Divisions. *Quarterly Journal of Economics*, 112(4), 1203-1250.

Honohan, P. (2008). Cross-Country Variation in Household Access to Financial Services. *Journal of Banking and Finance*, 32, 2493-2500.

Kamil, H., & Kulwant R. (2010). *The Global Credit Crunch and Foreign Banks' Lending to Emerging Markets: Why did Latin America Fare Better?* IMF working paper, 10/102.

Kaufmann, D., Aart K., and Massimo M. (2007). *Governance Matters VI: Governance Indicators of 1996-2006*. World Bank Policy Research Working Paper 4280, Washington, DC.

La Porta, R., Florencio L. S., Andrei S., and Robert W. V. (1997). Legal Determinants of External Finance, *Journal of Finance*, 52(3), 1131-1150.

La Porta, R., Florencio L. S., and Andrei S. (2002). Government Ownership of Banks. *Journal of Finance*, 57(1), 265-301.

Chapter 6

Shanghai Budapest Business Bridge

Roland Kapros [1], Agenlla Serafin [2]

Budapest College of Communication, Business and Arts Team

1   What Is a Global Financial Center?

A financial center is simply a location where a substantial amount of financial business is conducted. These centers come in different sizes and levels of capability, with no clear dividing line between a local financial center, a national one, a regional one, and a global one. Nonetheless, it is not that hard in practice to distinguish two global financial centers, London and New York, from the set of smaller regional and national financial centers that fall below them in the hierarchy, such as Frankfurt, Paris, or Singapore. Part of the difference is simply the scale of activity, which is much larger in the two global financial centers. More importantly, however, they are locations where a substantial amount of the business done has no inherent local connection. For example, if a Japanese company chooses to raise US dollars by issuing a bond in the London-based Eurodollar market, it is doing so in a foreign country and using a currency that is neither its own nor that of the country in which it is arranging the borrowing. The core reason for using London in this instance would be

---

[1] Roland Kapros is a junior student of Business Administration at Budapest College of Communication and Business.

[2] Agenlla Serafin is a senior student of International Economics at Budapest College of Communication and Business.

that the expertise and connections of the London investment banks will produce the funding on the best terms available in the global marketplace. A global financial center cannot attract such business without having a very high level of financial expertise, a full range of infrastructure, including globally-oriented law firms, a trusted legal system, and connections with a wide range of investors around the world. Other attributes are also important, as will be explored in the rest of this paper.

2   Why Do Financial Centers Exist in Our Electronic Age?

In this age of instant electronic communication, massive computer systems and databases, and electronic trading occurring literally in nanoseconds, one might wonder why financial systems have "centers" at all. The research literature does not fully address this core question, generally taking it as a given that such centers are necessary or listing essentially anecdotal points. This is an area where the author's two decades as an investment banker serve me in good stead, because I have seen and lived the reasons why having a center matters. The more lucrative and complex parts of finance are businesses where trust and confidence are absolutely critical. This matters, because humans evolved to communicate physically, using visual clues and even touch (such things as a firm handshake), to judge trustworthiness and the effectiveness of communication. Even in areas of finance where the minute-by-minute business is conducted by electronic means, the relationships that underlie those transactions are built through physical meetings, including informal outings to bars, restaurants, and sporting events. Further, finance is also an "apprenticeship" business in the sense that it is learned by paying close attention to one's bosses and mentors as they operate, rather than being something that can be easily learned in school. This requires being physically adjacent to the master banker, especially as this also allows informal interchanges where a novice can ask a master why he or she did something, or can benefit from a casual explanation that no one would bother to deliver by electronic means. For that matter, legal risks can arise when some points are written down or even spoken on a recorded line. (This is not to imply that illegal activities are common. The real problem is that the threat of lawsuits or investigations hangs over every transaction that might go wrong. A blunt comment about a bank's or a client's motivation or lack of understanding of an element of a transaction can be made to look quite damning in retrospect.) In sum, finance thrives on close physical contact even in this age of electronics and this is unlikely to change over the next decades, even if some of the less important aspects continue to migrate to electronic media. Therefore, "centers" will continue to matter. A small number of these centers will have the capacity to handle the most sophisticated or inherently global transactions and will rise to be truly global financial centers.

3 What Are the Benefits of Being Such a Center?

The most important and lucrative deals will occur where (1) the best bankers and traders will work there; (2) a host of ancillary businesses will make their main headquarters there in order to service the finance business, including lawyers, accountants, actuaries, specialist insurers, and many other professions; (3) the highly-paid professionals in finance and related businesses will employ many additional people to feed, clothe, house, entertain, and otherwise meet their needs; and the local currency will often be used as a matter of convenience in transactions.

4 General Attribute of Hungary

Located in East-Central Europe. The total population of Hungary is 10 million people. The capital is Budapest with 2 million people with suburbs almost 3.5 million people.

The business life is concentrated only in the capital city Budapest. Every highway and most of the long train networks connected to Budapest.

5 Why Budapest Could Be the Financial Center of East-Central Europe?

With great connections to Western Europe and the Balkans, we could say that Budapest can be the gate of Europe. Most of the qualified people speak English and other European languages for example: German, Italian, France, Spanish. Chinese language is becoming very popular now. Hungary's central location makes it a favourite destination for foreign investors who intend to expand their operations in central eastern Europe. The country's telecommunications, transport and logistics infrastructure, and the quality of education and life have attracted large amounts of foreign investment in Hungary in recent years. The capital, Budapest, is the center of the country's economic activity; however, the main cities are also gaining an increasing role. The country's favorable geographical location places it at the crossroads of main commercial routes. From Hungary, a market of some 250 million people can be reached within 600 miles (about 1,000 kilometers). EU accession in 2004 brought both commercial and regulatory advantages. Becoming an EU Member state brought a free trade system, the free movement of goods, services and labor, as well as capital. In addition to all these advantages, another of Hungary's strengths is its well-qualified labor force. Due to the high standards of its education system, the country has a highly-skilled and talented workforce, with professional foreign language skills and reasonably priced. Budapest is ideally located as a regional center for Central and Eastern Europe and is within easy reach of Western Europe. Communications and infrastructure are well developed; the work force is highly skilled. Budapest and Hungary have the best legal and financial infrastructure in the region. There is a relatively favorable tax environment. The level of corruption, while higher than desirable, is lower than in the neighboring countries.

5.1 Financial sector

The legal background of the Hungarian financial sector and the relevant regulations substantially follow the European Union directives and standards. The regulation of the financial sector is in full conformity with the EU regulations. All major laws relating to banking, insurance, securities, mutual funds and private pension funds conform to EU legislation.

5.2 Banking and finance

Banks followed by other financial institutions and enterprises can provide the widest range of financial services in Hungary. Foreign-owned banks dominate the Hungarian banking sector. At the beginning of the year 2000, Hungary had one of the healthiest banking and financial systems in the central European region. The recent financial crisis hit the Hungarian banking sector severely. The lending dropped significantly both for individuals and SMEs (Small and medium enterprises)

5.3 Human resources

Now in Budapest, there are 400,000 students in 70 higher education institutions, among them, 100,000 majoring in business administration faculties, 90% of students speak English, 20% of fresh graduates have international experience, 61% of students have professional experience, and seniors and executives with several years of experience are readily available.

Many corporate executives agree that foreign language skills in Hungary have generally improved significantly in the last ten years. A pool of highly educated multilingual working are available especially between the ages of 20 and 30.

5.4 Quality of life

Foreigners and investors generally find Hungary to be as open and friendly. The majority of the expatriate community considers Budapest to be a pleasant place to live. The expatriate community leads a very active social life. Although the housing conditions are relatively good and affordable in Budapest for all levels of business managers, the surveyed noted that there is a big gap in the quality of life between the capital city and the countryside, even in the case of larger towns. The outlook of the city has been improved through the refurbishment of many buildings. The crime rate is relatively low, although in some areas — especially car theft — need further improvement.

5.5 Taxation

The base rate of corporate tax is 19%, however with a tax base of 500 million HUF the tax rate is only 10%. The general VAT rate is 27%. In 2012 the government has accepted the Job Protection Action Plan. This scheme offers a simplified taxation especially for micro companies. Additionally, it enhances the employment of those social groups which are the most vulnerable by providing cuts from their social contributions. Since the SME sector provides the majority of private sphere employment therefore it benefits the most from the Job Protection Action Plan. In 2013 super-grossing has been abolished, thus a proportionate, flat-rate personal income taxation system has been introduced: the rate of tax is uniformly and transparently 16% on every type of a private person's income. As a result of the Job Protection Action Plan companies can receive cuts from the social contributions if they employ people from the most vulnerable social groups. By 2013 the share of taxes and contributions payable on labor within total tax revenues is expected to get below the ratio of revenues from levies on sales and consumption as well as wealth taxes.

5.6 Education

Executives surveyed mostly agreed that the Hungarian workforce is well educated. In the IT and technology sector, the educational level was deemed to be especially good, many times above the international average. It was stressed, however, that the government does have a key role to play in financing the education system, an area of concern today. A critical factor to improved education is more competitive salaries for teachers, and university professors. The corporate executives welcomed that the universities started to focus on the needs of the business sector, training sufficient students in appropriate areas to meet market demands and not according to the head-quota financing policy of the government. Corporations and associations are working with the universities and government to jointly assess the market projections for various major fields of study.

5.7 Infrastructure

Hungary's geographic position naturally lends itself to the establishment of Logistic & Distribution hubs for international trade. This position should be exploited in every aspect (shipping on the Danube, forwarding on the roads and rails or by aircraft). The EU Cohesion Fund provides financial sources for large infrastructure development projects which took place in the last 8 years. As a result the highway network developed significantly. Regarding IT and Telecom in Hungary there is no problem with availability of the highest technological level of IT & Telecom services. Since most of the corporations which provide these services are present in the country, many have in fact already established their regional centers here.

5.8 Securities market

The Budapest Stock Exchange and all issuers of shares are regulated by rules that are in line with European Union standards. The integration of the regional capital market is ongoing. The general economic conditions are not favorable for a dynamic capital market development. Government bonds however represent a significant part of the trade. Although the current crisis detracts from Budapest's position as a possible regional financial center, according to some corporate executives it remains a possible opportunity for Budapest on a long run.

Predictability and credibility are key factors in the government's economic policy. A strong economic leadership is needed in order to position the country and re-engineer economic policy, imbedding a consequent economic and social responsibility, targeting the vision of Budapest as a regional business center of central and eastern Europe.

5.9 Legal environment

As Hungary is part of the European Union, most of its business legislation is adopted from EU legislation. Membership thus provides a strong and reliable legal environment and it makes it easier for companies to extend their operations to other EU members. The most important changes in the legal environment have been implemented by the current government. By 2013 the most essential modifications of the tax system has already taken place and there has been a new labor Code implemented. The new Penal Code will enter into force on July 1, 2013 and the new Civil Code is planned to come into force in 2014. As a result, the reform of the legal environment will be finalized by 2014.

5.10 Growth and fiscal stability

Both in Hungary and in Europe the most important challenge will be the return to growth and increasing employment while still maintaining a strong fiscal discipline. It is of utmost importance to maintain budget control in order to provide a stable economic environment. The reforms implemented in the previous years provide solid bases for new, employment led economic growth in Hungary. In case the macroeconomic conditions improve in the European Union, there will be a fierce competition to benefit from the growth of the West. Therefore, increasing competitiveness of the economy is essential so the domestic economy can also utilize the improving European economic performance.

6 Plan: Budapest Gate

The 100,000 sqm office park in Örmező is located at the " west gate of Budapest" where the largest multi-modal transportation junction of Hungary is under development. Visitors coming by train, or by car on the highways will get their first impression of the city of Budapest by looking at Budapest Gate Office Park with the Buda hills in their background.

The area has unique transportation facilities: Direct links to motorway M1 and M7, the future terminal station of metro line 4, direct connection with Kelenföld Railway Station with the Vienna Intercity access, the terminal stations of 10 inner city buses and 2 tram lines.

With straight connection to the Etele City Center, the full range of services and shops will make everyday life more comfortable for the tenants. Relaxation will be served by the extensive green areas surrounding the buildings, restaurants, cafés as well as additional retail and service units.

The offices are planned to be added with underground parking places for 1,000 cars.

7 Shanghai-Budapest Business Bridge

Hungary is a very open economy, therefore it is crucial to create an economic climate which increases competitiveness and also protects the domestic economy from outside shocks. For the latter, the government has created a 500 billion HUF strategic reserve in the 2013 budget. In order to promote competitiveness, the government has introduced several measures which will first show results in 2013, like the administrative burden reduction program for companies, the Job Protection Action Plan, the new free enterprise zones and stimulation of R&D activities.

One of the competitive advantages Hungary has compared to other countries in the region is the government's strong commitment to easing business processes and to increasing the competitiveness of both SMEs and large enterprises in Hungary based on the wide range of available incentives. Both refundable and nonrefundable incentives are available to investors coming to or expanding in Hungary. The main types of incentives related to investments are cash subsidies either from the Hungarian Government or from EU Funds, tax incentives, low-interest loans, or land available free or at reduced prices. The regulations on incentive opportunities are in accordance with EU rules.

The region's largest Chinese community lives in Hungary, the Bank of China has established a subsidiary in Budapest, and big companies such as Asia Center operate in Budapest.

Hungarian experts pointed out that setting up plants in Hungary would allow Chinese companies to escape EU anti-dumping procedures that currently, affect goods coming from China.

There are specific opportunities where economic cooperation between the two countries would be highly beneficial; these include setting up solar cell and electronic devices manufacturing plants. But, there are excellent opportunities in producing traditional Chinese medicine in Hungary, setting up joint electronic vehicle manufacturing plants and developing health and spa tourism industries.

International companies often concentrate some of their corporate service activities in regional centers (Corporate HQ, IT services, Logistics, Corporate Finance, Customer Service Center etc.) according to their organizational structure. The selection of such macro-regional center depends on various factors (quality of life, regional vs. local business volume, market regulations, legal environment, business climate, business culture etc.) and the changes in business strategy of the companies often result in establishing such a center, to dissolve it, or renew it according to their needs.

According to a survey carried out in 2001 (with the support of the Ministry of Economy and the AMCHAM in Hungary) among foreign businesses in Hungary, 69% of the companies had one or the other type of regional center (Figure 6-1), and 44% of them had them already in Budapest (Figure 6-2) or in other parts of the country. Budapest was followed by Vienna with 24%-al (see the 2001 Conference Final Report page 4)

Those companies having regional centers have the type of the centers as follows: 76% regional headquarters, 64% IT services, 52% HR, 48% R&D, Accounting 44%. (Figure 6-3)

Most of the executives surveyed agree that Budapest has a great potential to be the host of regional corporate centers, especially given the high forecast economic growth of the region.

7.1 Connection, friendship between the cultures

The Hungarian Cultural Institute will open in Beijing this year and the government is determined to increase the number of Chinese students accepted in Hungarian Universities under the mutual scholarships

Figure 6-1 Does the company have regional center?

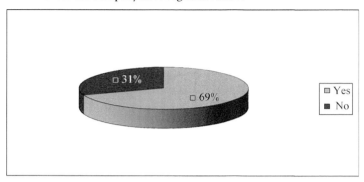

Figrue 6-2 If yes, in which city?

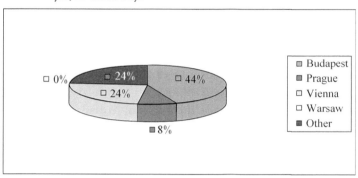

Figure 6-3 If yes, in which activities/divisions?

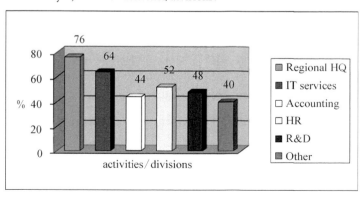

agreement signed by the two governments.

China is Hungary's largest trade partner outside the European Union. Hungary is the largest destination for Chinese investments in Central and Eastern Europe.

7.2   Chinese companies and banks

Huawei Technologies, a leading information and communication technology solutions provider, agreed to set up a logistics center in Hungary.

ZTE signed an agreement with the Hungarian government to set up an operating maintenance center in Hungary that would target consumers across Europe.

China's Zhuzhou Times New Material Tech. Co. plans to establish a base in Hungary to sell earthquake resistant building technology in European markets, the National Innovation Office (NIH) said on Wednesday. The base isolation technology was developed with the assistance of a Hungarian professor, Emanuel Csorba.

The first Bank of China branch in Hungary opened 9 years ago. The institution has remained committed to promoting trade between the two countries and supporting the local economy, whose efforts have won the backing and recognition of the communities in Hungary. The opening of a second branch in Budapest pointed to a new step of the BOC to expand its operation in Hungary. It showed the BOC's confidence in Hungary. The branches would play a more active role in promoting economic ties and financial cooperation between China and Hungary as well as the whole of central and eastern Europe.

7.3   Agreements between China and Hungary

China Civil Engineering Construction Corp signed a memorandum worth $1 billion on building a 20-kilometer rail express linking the airport to downtown Budapest.

As part of the seven cooperative deals, the commerce and agriculture ministries signed cooperative memorandums on cooperation of small and medium-sized enterprises and cooperation in agriculture. China Development Bank signed an agreement with the Hungarian government on a financial framework.

The Budapest financial Center helps the Chinese companies to get inside the EU. There are good employment conditions for Chinese people, and the Chinese who live in Hungary are very well-integrated into the Hungarian culture. They won Hungarian talent competition as well. Speaking and learning Chinese is becoming popular these days. There is a Chinese major at one of the Universities as well.

National Economy Minister Mihály Varga today announced an agreement on a €100 million credit line between the state-owned Export-Import Bank (Eximbank) and its Chinese counterpart. In announcing the agreement, Varga stated that the agreement was designed primarily for Hungarian companies seeking to export to China.

A biennial meeting of the Chinese-Hungarian Science and Technology Joint Committee in Beijing has taken decisions on almost 40 joint applications, National Innovation Office deputy chief László Korányi told MTI on Wednesday. The 36 Chinese-Hungarian applications for funding were picked from 59, Korányi said. The Hungarian contribution for the funding was €1 million.

7.4 A vibrant city

Budapest is the commercial center of Hungary, which opens many business opportunities as alluded to previously. In addition, the city has a range of entertainment, dining, and cultural options that could be attractive to many expatriates as well as Hungarian nationals.

8 Conclusion

We perceived that Budapest has a great potential to be the financial and business center of Central and South-eastern Europe. The main issues which we addressed concern Budapest's and Hungary's current and potential future position including identifying competitive edges, key competencies of the economic environment, importance of the pool of highly qualified workforce, cost of labor, quality of life, and regulatory environment.

References

Arner, D. W. (2009). *The Competition of International Financial Centers and the Role of Law*. In Karl M. Meessen, (ed.). Economic Law as an Economic Good: Its Rule Function and its Tool Function in the Competition of Systems. Sellier.

Bertaud, A. (2004). *The Spatial Organization of Cities: Deliberate Outcome or Unforeseen Consequence?* Institute of Urban & Regional Development. IURD Working Paper Series. Paper WP-2004-01.

Kindleberger, C. P. (1974). The Formation of Financial Centers: A Study in Comparative Economic History. *Princeton Studies in International Finance*, Princeton University Press: Princeton, New Jersey.

Sassen, S. (1999). Global Financial Centers. Foreign Affairs. January/February.

Tschoegl, A. E. (2000). International Banking Centers, Geography, and Foreign Banks, Financial Markets. *Institutions & Instruments*, 9(1), 1-32.

Parr, J. D. (1978). Models of the Central Place System: A More General Approach. *Urban Studies*, 15, 35-49.

http://repositories.cdlib.org/iurd/wps/WP-2004-01.

http://www.tervlap.hu/cikk/show/id/1871.

http://www.realdeal.hu/20120110/are-developer-futureals-future-plans-for-real/.

http://www.brookings.edu/~/media/research/files/papers/2011/6/10%20shanghai%20financial%20center%20elliott/0610_shanghai_financial_center_elliott.

http://www.futureal.hu/en/gate_of_budapest.php.

http://www.bbj.hu/business/chinese-company-plans-to-use-hungary-as-base_65643.

http://www.chinacham.hu/hirek/page/4.

http://www.bibca.net/en/home.

http://privatbankar.hu/kkv/kinaban-sem-tarthato-fenn-a-vegtelensegig-a-ketszamjegyu-novekedes-interju-251056.

Chapter 7

Turning Taipei into an International Financial Center

Shou-Han Liu[1], En-Ti Hwang [2] Tien-Yung Chou[3], Shao-Yi Peng[4]

National Taiwan University Team

Coach: Dar-Yeh Hwang[*]

1 What Is an International Financial Center?

Usually, the international financial center is the center of financial capital, financial institutions and financial information with the attributes of low transaction costs, high trading volume and transaction efficiency. The international finance center comprises typically various financial markets, including money market, foreign exchange market,

---

[1] Shou-Han Liu is an undergraduate majoring in Finance at National Taiwan University.
[2] En-Ti Hwang is an undergraduate majoring in Chemical Engineering at National Taiwan University.
[3] Tien-Yung Chou is an undergraduate majoring in Finance at National Taiwan University.
[4] Shao-Yi Peng is an undergraduate majoring in Finance at National Taiwan University.
[*] Dar Yeh Hwang is a professor in Department of Finance and Dep. of Journalism at National Taiwan University. He received his doctorate of finance from Rutgers University. He is chairman of Banking Education Association of Taiwan, and the Dean of the Academy of Promoting Economic Legislation.

bond market, stock market, futures market and other establishment in this place and develops freely, efficiently carries out all kinds of financial transactions.

The Essential conditions of international finance center are relatively strong economic strength; a stable political, economic environment with efficient market mechanism; highly concentrated financial institutions and developed financial markets, with high efficiency for mobilization and funds; sound financial regulations and management system; sufficient financial professionals, strategic location, convenient transportation, with modern communication facilities and other supporting ancillary services as well.

2 Taiwan

Taiwan region is located in eastern Asia, northwest side of the Pacific with a population of more than 23 million, and its total area is about 36,000 square kilometers. The average annual economic growth rate is about 8% in the past 30 years, while export-oriented policies provide proficient foreign exchange. Taiwan's foreign exchange reserves are the world's sixth. According to the ROC DGBAS statistics, per capita GNP in 1961 was $153, and over $20,000 in 2011. Taiwan has annual per capita income of over thirty thousand U.S. dollars by purchasing power parity, which is comparable to the world's major advanced regions. Current annual per capita income: (2012 international exchange rate) $20,364/(2012 PPP/IMF data) $38,486.

3 Why Can We Turn Taipei into an International Financial Center?

Geographic location

Taiwan region locates in eastern Asia, northwest side of the Pacific, so people here can easily interact with other countries such as Japan, Korea, India, Philippine, Australia, etc. However, people in the west also come to Taiwan to develop their business because of its friendliness and open policy.

Traffic

Being a strong financial center, Taiwan's domestic and international traffic plays an important role. It boosts Taiwan Railways Administration, Taiwan High Speed Rail, Taipei Metro Rail Transportation (MRT) and international airports, such as Taiwan Taoyuan International Airport, Taipei Songshan Airport, and Kaohsiung International Airport. Also, MRT is highly developed and it will get further development and be more convenient in recent years. Hence, this is an important advantage for Taiwan to be an international financial market.

ECFA

The Economic Cooperation Framework Agreement (ECFA) is a preferential trade agreement between Chinese mainland and Taiwan that aims to reduce tariffs and commercial barriers between the two sides. The ECFA, signed on June 29, 2010, in Chongqing, was seen as the most significant agreement since 1949. It will boost the current US$110 billion bilateral trade between both sides.

Benefit to TW

The ECFA has been compared with the Closer Economic Partnership Arrangements Chinese mainland signed with the Special Administrative Regions: Hong Kong and Macau.

The deal is thought to be structured to benefit the Taiwan region far more than Chinese mainland. The "early harvest" list of tariff concessions covers 539 Taiwanese products and 267 mainland Chinese goods. The advantage to Taiwan region would amount to US$13.8 billion, while Chinese mainland would receive benefits estimated at US$2.86 billion. The Chinese mainland will also open its markets in 11 service sectors such as banking, securities, insurance, hospitals and accounting, while Taiwan region agreed to offer wider access in seven areas, including banking and movies.

Language and culture advantage

We all knew that the biggest international financial centers in the world are located in London, Tokyo, and, of course, Shanghai. We speak Chinese in our daily life, and Chinese has become one of the most powerful languages recently. People in Taiwan study English since they are seven years old or even earlier. And Japan is a popular country in Taiwan region, so many people can speak Japanese here. We can interact with these important countries and learn much from their experiences in establishing an international financial center.

Education

People in Taiwan go to school from seven to eighteen. And nearly 99% students will keep studying in colleges. We have many talented people to turn Taipei into an international financial center.

History of Taiwan as the world's sixth largest foreign exchange reserves

1974–1979	The permission of interest difference between banks
1979–1985	Establish deposit rates in freedom at the maximum interest rate, set the basic loan system, formulate the interest difference based on credit rating
1985–1990	Cancel the limitation of deposit interest rate gradually

All financial related companies such as banking, securities, life insurance and property insurance, are controlled by a major financial holding company.

First financial reform

Recently, Taiwan region administrative leader Ma Ying-jeou met with "Academy of Promoting Economic Legislation" scholars Dar-Yeh Huang and others, listening to their views on fiscal and financial issues. Dar-Yeh Huang urges to actively promote financial reform in Taiwan region, and Ma promised to refer the issues related to the Executive Yuan for reference.

Ma Ying-jeou pointed out that the financial policy focused on reference to the supervision of domestic measures in order to help provide enterprises in international business opportunities to develop overseas. This policy will also strengthen the Capital Adequacy and implementation of Risk Management mechanisms continuously to maintain market stability.

After the meeting, Dar-Yeh Huang, Dean of "Academy of Promoting Economic Legislation" , paraphrased that he suggested to promote financial reform earlier including the establishment of the reform group and motivating the banks for public to release shares operation.

Dar-Yeh Huang relayed that Ma attached great importance to the financial reform agenda, but the reform was the responsibility of Executive Yuan. Dar-Yeh Huang said the declaration of "528 financial reform" attracted thousands of financial operators, elected representatives as well as the support of experts and scholars, so he expected to announce the promotion as soon as possible after this meeting.

There are four main demands of "528 Financial Reform", including (i) the Executive Yuan shall establish an interagency group on financial reforms in order to implement financial reform goals; (ii) the government should guarantee the continuity of the financial policies, and ensure they will not be influenced by the change of ruling parties or supervisors; (iii) the pure public sector banks are responsible for implementation of national policies only; (iv) accelerate to release shares of private banks, but the process must be open and transparent.

In fact, the Executive Yuan had conducted a comprehensive review when Ma took office, but the emergence of continuity has still not been paid enough attention to. Nowadays, the cross-strait financial situation Changes rapidly. Dar-Yeh Huang believed that if Ma had vigorously promoted the financial reform of domestic banks five years ago, the scene of Taiwan's financial market and the competitive ability of Taiwan banks would have gone far away. Dar-Yeh Huang claimed that the promoting of financial reform is at a critical moment in history, in order to restore the long-lost public support, Ma must carry out the financial reform in full swing.

Second financial reform

Due to promoting the establishment of three financial institutions in Taiwan region by (2005), and increasing the market share, the number of holding company in Taiwan region halved from 14 down to 7 by 2005.

How to turn Taipei into an international financial center? The following criteria must be met: favorable operating conditions, tax incentives, education and training, Asia Pacific Market, strengthening and expanding the economic scale, encouraging innovation, strengthening risk management, the RMB liberalization, and financial deregulation.

Chapter 8

The Development and Future of Shanghai as an International Financial Center

LING Quincy[1], OSWALD Kolja[2], TURNBULL Mahoney[3]
Matariki University Network Team
Coach: Zhiyao Zhang[*]

1 Introduction

An international financial center (IFC) is a key component of an economic superpower's ability to maximize its role in the global economy. The seminal literature on the concept of financial centers — pioneered by Kindleberger (1973) — emphasizes the role of an IFC in marshalling and streamlining financial resources and transactions within a nation-state for subsequent outward and inward flows to and from the broader global economy, respectively.

---

[1] Ling Quincy is a junior in School of Law at Fudan University.
[2] Oswald Kolja is a student of Business Administration and Management at University of Baltimore, and also an editor for Innovative China.com.
[3] Mahoney Turnbull comes from New Zealand and have been studying at Fudan University on an exchange for one semester. Whilst in Shanghai she undertook an internship with King & Wood Mallesons law firm, as well as a New Zealand Dairy company in which is related to my prior research experience on sustainable agriculture. She is a Young Leader in the "Asia New Zealand" network and I am engaged in promoting stronger links in the Asia Pacific region, with China as the key focus.
[*] Zhiyao Zhang is the director of Queen's China Liaison Officer, and the Adjunct Professor of Fudan University. After he earned his PhD in political science from Jilin University in 1990s, he received another doctorate from Queen's University.

Kindleberger (1973) has highlighted how an IFC plays a fundamental economic role, as well as more niche roles related to international finance, "financial centers are needed not only to balance the savings and investments of individual entrepreneurs through time, and to transfer finance capital from savers to investors, but to effect payments and transfer savings over distance… The specialized functions of international payments and foreign lending or borrowing are typically best performed by one central place which is also the specialized center for domestic interregional payments."

Thus, an IFC functions as a central hub within a country. It becomes, through either formal or informal means, "above" all others in importance or prestige. Moreover, by virtue of this national role, it also functions as the key access point between the nation and foreign sources of commerce, whether these sources are markets, investors, or inward and outward foreign direct investment (FDI).

Shanghai's Lujiazui Central Finance District plays this role within China. As Shanghai comes into its own as a financial center, and accumulates its IFC "qualifications" and the associated global importance and prestige, the city can alleviate the difficulties associated with this ascension by studying how other centers have accomplished the same feat. This paper focuses on the rise and development of the international financial center (IFC) of Shanghai, examining the future challenges that will arise from establishing this IFC, and strategies that may support Shanghai evolving into a global IFC. Frankfurt's IFC is used as case study, to compare Frankfurt's development, in order to gain potential insights on where Shanghai could be heading. While no two cities, circumstances or eras, are the same, it is our contention that Frankfurt provides an excellent example to contrast with Shanghai, in order to explore the elements and possibilities inherent in creating and maintaining a prosperous IFC.

First, we will introduce Frankfurt and its IFC as a case study and discuss its development. Then we will introduce Shanghai and its IFC and talk about its development, its status quo, and finally leading into an analysis on what areas of the Shanghai IFC can be improved using Tschoegl's four dimensional models (2000). As is visible by the table below, Frankfurt is a suitable case study to compare Shanghai with, as it also has a large International Financial Center, and is a major stakeholder in the world of finance.

Ranking	International Financial centers Development Index (2012)	Worldwide centers of Commerce Index (2008)	Global Financial centers Index (2013)
1st	New York	London	London
2nd	London	New York	New York
3rd	Tokyo	Tokyo	Hong Kong
4th	Hong Kong	Singapore	Singapore
5th	Singapore	Chicago	Seoul
6th	Shanghai	Hong Kong	Tokyo
7th	Frankfurt	Paris	Boston
8th	Paris	Frankfurt	Zurich
9th	Zurich	Seoul	Genf
10th	Chicago	Amsterdam	Frankfurt
24th		Shanghai	
21st			Shanghai

2 Methodologies

In order to assess the IFC's of Frankfurt and Shanghai in an effective manner, we have used Tschoegls four dimensional model of financial centers. Tschoegl describes financial centers as primary markets where financial capital is collected, switched, disbursed and exchanged. Tschoegl divides financial centers into four dimensions.

i) Governments, financial and non-financial corporations, individuals, and retail customers.

APPROACHES AND CHALLENGES

ii) The second dimension is geographic reach of an IFC; where a financial center can be distinguished between domestic, regional, interregional, and global centers.

iii) The third dimension includes the products, and the range of services that the stakeholders of an IFC have to offer.

iv) The fourth dimension is the value-added chain, which describes the level of know-how of an IFC.

This conceptual framework can be shown the following way:

	Clients	Geographic Reach	Products	Value-added Chain
Variables	Central Bank Capital of country HQ of domestic banks Regional HQ of foreign banks Branches and subsidiaries of foreign banks Domestic listed companies Foreign listed companies Employees in financial services Port	Domestic vs. regional vs. inter-regional vs. global financial center Offshore vs. Onshore center Mobility Communication infrastructure International promotion	Regulation Banks Capital Markets	Value-added per employee Talent pool Universities Level of research

As many scholars have used this model in regards to IFC's around the world, we have used Boering and Loechel's work from 2010 as a reference, where they also crafted a Tschoegls model for both Shanghai and Frankfurt (Appendix 1.1 and 1.2), in a very comprehensive manner. We have used Boering and Loechel's comprehensive analysis and identified the key aspects of each dimension that are particularly relevant to the future development of the Shanghai IFC, in the sense that they may keep Shanghai from developing into a successful global IFC. We have thus created a new Tschoegls model, which has enabled us to analyze each financial center in a structured and well-founded manner, giving us a sound foundation from which to investigate the respective financial centers.

3   Frankfurt as a Case Study

In order to look at Frankfurt as a case study and draw implications from it, first the development and history of the IFC of Frankfurt needs to be discussed.

3.1   The development and history of Frankfurt as an IFC

After World War II, Germany was structurally and economically devastated, and had a lot of developing to do. Part of the groundwork that had to be done in order to redevelop Germany, included forming a financial center. Germans had to decide where to place the financial center geographically. Contenders for this IFC were Düsseldorf, Hamburg and Frankfurt. Even though Düsseldorf and Hamburg seemed to be more likely choices, Frankfurt ended up winning the race, even though not considered a predominant center of its country at that time. Düsseldorf and Hamburg both were major economic stakeholders at that time, and Frankfurt's proximity to the US military base ended up being the decisive factor as to why Frankfurt became the IFC in Germany.

Part of becoming the IFC in Germany, also included establishing the central bank in Frankfurt. Today the central bank of Germany, the Deutsche Bundesbank is considered as the most important European central bank, after the ECB respectively, which is also located in Frankfurt. Frankfurt is considered as a second tier financial center, and has less magnitude in Europe than London. After the establishment of the Frankfurt stock exchange in the early 1960s, most foreign banks settled in Frankfurt in order to be in close proximity to the stock market. At that time it was of great importance to be geographically close to the stock market, if one wanted to trade effectively. In addition, the German payment settlement system was located close to Frankfurt, meaning that if one wanted to conduct business efficiently, it was of great advantage to be located in and around Frankfurt. Hence, the number of foreign banks present in Frankfurt greatly increased at that time, with an increase from about 40 to about 180 foreign banks settling in Frankfurt.

After the German reunification, many people questioned whether Berlin would become the new financial center of Germany. Frankfurt's share of German representative offices did decline after the reunification, and there was a shared belief that Berlin would arise as new financial center, however this trend never effectively followed through, and as of present Berlin plays a slim role in the financial sector.

Over recent years a strong trend has been visible in regards to Frankfurt's IFC. As strong as the increase of concentration of banks was in Frankfurt after the establishment of the IFC, banks are now moving out of Frankfurt. Researchers call this trend the inverted "U — Curve", and attribute this trend to a number of reasons. First of all geographical proximity comes into play. Banks seem to establish their subsidiaries close to their headquarters. The importance of this is that since Germany has a lot of neighboring countries, and these countries have subsidiaries in Germany, banks from neighboring countries tend to settle in German cities close to their headquarters. This is especially visible in the case of Austrian banks, where 13 of 18 Austrian banks that conduct business in Germany, have established their subsidiaries in Bavaria. The second major reason for a decrease in bank establishments in Frankfurt has been the development of Information and Communication Technology (ICT). With the development of ICT, it is less important to be geographically close to the financial center you are conducting business with. Due to the modern support available, business can be easily conducted on a global scale through ICT. This is highlighted in the financial sector with the use of computer based trading, which allows individuals to trade from anywhere in the world. The prevalence of computer based trading is a universal trend and can be seen in IFCs around the world, however this does not threaten the existence of IFC's as certain financial services still require a fundamentally physical presence. These services include high-end and high-complex financial services, where there are either large sums at stake, or high complexity deals, both times when it is critical for parties to meet face-to-face in order to facilitate the best transaction possible. Another instance in which ICT cannot be relied upon to generate success is in the context of customer service. Banks are increasingly using customer service as competitive advantage. As bank operations often include handling sizeable amounts of money, customer service is safer when done face-to-face, rather than on the phone or on the internet.

3.2 Implications

As Frankfurt's economic landscape is quite different to Shanghais, and Shanghai aims to become a global IFC instead of an interregional one, which Frankfurt is, it is uncertain as to what extent Frankfurt's IFC development is comparable to Shanghai's. However, a few past trends can be taken under consideration, as they will influence Shanghai's IFC, even if not in the exact same manner (Grote, 2008).

Firstly, Frankfurt's battle with other cities, especially with Berlin, the capital demonstrates that the capital does not necessarily need to be the financial center. Undoubtedly, Shanghai is in a more complicated situation, as the capital is not only Beijing, but also most domestic bank's headquarters and the central bank are in Beijing. Within China, Shanghai's role as absolute financial center should be emphasized and backed by all government stakeholders, in order to create a clear power structure.

Furthermore, probably the most important development of Frankfurt's IFC in regards to Shanghai's IFC is the decrease of jobs in Frankfurt due to the development of ICT. As stated above, in its nature the development of ICT does not threaten the existence of IFC's, but decreases the need for low-skill labor. Hence, Shanghai should take this universal trend under consideration, and from the beginning have a strategy to create a high-complex and a high-end financial services industry, where the development of ICT is used as a support technology, instead of threatening jobs (Grote, 2008).

4 Shanghai as an IFC

In order to examine Shanghai as an International Financial, a close look at the history and past development is important.

4.1 The development and history of Shanghai as an IFC

The origins

To understand the culmination of Shanghai's IFC project, one must first understand the origins and development of the Lujiazui Central Finance District in Pudong. The growth and maturation of the district have indeed mirrored that of Shanghai itself, and policy decisions regarding the organization and structure of Lujiazui help explain Shanghai's rapid emergence as a global financial center. These policy decisions originated from both the national central government and the Shanghai Municipal Government (SMG). In 1992, Deng Xiaoping stated that, "Shanghai used to be a financial center where people exchanged currency freely, and it should continue to serve as the center. To attain an international seat in banking, China has to rely on Shanghai first" (Olds, 1997). So it is clear that developing Shanghai into a global financial center was a keystone of China's overall modernization and development strategy. Indeed, the broader trends affecting China, like the end of Maoism in the late 1970s and the New Open Door Policy of the 1980s, cannot be decoupled from Shanghai's emergence, as the city was used strategically to spearhead and accelerate many of the economic reforms. To create the space and environment for Lujiazui to emerge as a viable engine of Shanghai's economic preeminence, the SMG relied on "a mix of policies to relocate industrial development out of the central city, reduce population density in the central city, attract FDI and other forms of overseas capital (e.g. debt), attract foreign technology, and attract management skills and knowledge about development strategies" (Olds,

1997). These were the first steps in restructuring the city similar to how Hong Kong, Singapore, Tokyo, and New York remade themselves in the 20th century. A boom in infrastructure changes and improvements occurred in the 1990s, all geared towards creating an environment within Lujiazui that would lure and facilitate commerce. These included:

Construction of the Nanpu and Yangpu bridges over the Huangpu River
Construction of inner and outer ring roads
Construction of two subway lines
Construction of tunnels under the Huangpu river
A major upgrade of Shanghai's Waigaoqiao port
Construction of the Pudong airport
Dramatically improved telecommunications infrastructure
National fiber optic cable network
Digital celluar network
6 million square meters of new housing

So people who only know the Shanghai of 2010 and later may take the modernity of the city for granted, but the list above illustrates how Lujiazui was in many ways the main impetus for much of the modern infrastructure associated with contemporary Shanghai. At the same time physical infrastructure was being upgraded, other "reform-oriented initiatives" were also being enacted: "(1) the opening up of Shanghai's financial markets; (2) land reform; and (3) the formation of development zones, including the nationally sanctioned Pudong New Area project. Lujiazui Central Finance District in Pudong is a creature of the intersection of these initiatives" (Olds, 1997). The Pudong project was a boon for Lujiazui because it brought national attention and resources to bear on the project, as national economic development and urbanization were recognized to be inseparable phenomena by the Chinese central government. So-called "zhongdian chengshi" — or "key-point" cities — were targeted, and Shanghai was certainly one of the most prominent. So both nationally and internationally, Shanghai was designated as a critical component of China's identity and future prosperity.

In some ways the objective has been to make Shanghai a Manhattan of the 21st century, with Lujiazui "conceptualized as an international standard 'landing strip' to 'lure in' deregulated 'foreign finance capital to build the office space that would lure major financial institutions to set up' operations" (Olds, 1997). In 1986, the SMG released its Shanghai Master Plan, which focused on these objectives. France's Institut d'Amanagement et d'Urbanisme de la Region Ile de France (IAURIF) greatly influenced this document— a trend that would be continued via consulting agreements between the SMG and French consultancy firms dealing with Lujiazui. In 1990, China's central government officially opened the Pudong Special Economic Zone (SEZ), and the SMG felt pressure to accelerate the pace of development. Furthermore, it was obvious that the outcome of the project would be scrutinized on a national — and indeed international — level, so the end result had to be visually appealing and modern. Lujiazui "needed to act as 'an important symbol and image of the results of reform' and the 'successes' of the New Open Door Policy." So it was more than just a development project in this regard; there was symbolism associated with China's national pride and increased role in the 21st century global economy too.

In 1991, Shanghai former Mayor Zhu Rongji visited the Ministry of Public Engineering in Paris, where he signed an agreement opening up the Lujiazui development to international consultation and competition, accepting technical and financial assistance from France for the project. The design competition "was viewed by the SMG as a meditated publicity show, a discursive event which would raise the international profile of Lujiazui and Pudong... used to hook Shanghai up to the flows of capital and technology shifting around the world" (Olds,1997) Ultimately, five completing plans were narrowed down to three finalists. The plans included "recommendations [that] dealt with transportation issues, green space, urban form, the feasibility of phased implementation, urban vitality, the historical context, future changes in information and technology, links with other districts, program planning, administration of the zone, and recommendations for the next stage" (Olds 1997).

Merging into a global player

Shanghai has emerged into a global city over a relatively short period of time. It was only ten years ago that Wu (2003) noted how, "According to standards in the literature, Shanghai should not be considered a global city. The city rarely appears in the list of global cities such as New York, London, and Tokyo," and it would technically fall into the category of a "globalizing city." But after a decade of development projects, urbanization, a deluge of foreign capital, and the emergence of Shanghai's port as busiest in the world, Shanghai is indisputably a global city. It is our contention that systematic planning by local and national governments, developers, and business leaders accounts for this rapid evolution. Furthermore, we assert that self-reinforcing dynamics are at play, whereby Shanghai would not have developed an IFC without this meteoric growth, and this meteoric growth would not have occurred without the development of an IFC. It is "place promotion" that accounts for this paradoxical phenomenon. With place promotion, local authorities take a proactive approach to urban development, seeking to improve the image of their locality and lure businesses and development projects. According to Wu (2003), the SMG's promotion strategy included "a wide range of policies such as the designation of development zones (e.g., Economic and Technological Development Zones and Free Trade Zones), preferential treatment of investors, land-leasing instruments to facilitate land use changes, key infrastructure projects, and direct investment in urban development." The policies burnished the reputation of Shanghai as an up and coming metropolitan area in the mid-2000s, and it amounted to investment and methodical development of an IFC, which in turn spawned further interest and investment in the city. Increased interest and investment in the city served to bolster the IFC itself, and it is in this manner that the self-reinforcing pendulum alluded to above began to swing. "The SMG used various high-profile conferences, exhibitions, and international planning consultants to promote a new image of Shanghai. In particular, the planning of the Lujiazui Finance and Trade Zone attracted wide media attention." (Wu, 2003)

A new image

Shanghai is the gateway of China to the global economy and frontier of globalization. Shanghai has been described as the origin of China's modern manufacturing industry and financial business. As such, Shanghai is the frontier of a rigorously planned economy to interface with the broader global economy; China's main economic channel connected to the globalized world. The connection between subsidized production factors and the production capacity is broken. Shanghai's utilization of foreign investment reflects stronger international influences than in the Pearl River delta. Investment in Shanghai represents more than the simple utilization of cheap labor. The model is turning from industrial surplus to property-led development. The new urban image is depicted as a pro-growth city that is more willing to listen to the market signals rather than planning requirements. But, as in many other places, urban development in Shanghai is deeply embedded in the political economy of place. However, Shanghai is trying to find a way out of the dilemma. Yang Xiong, Shanghai mayor, once announced that Shanghai's free trade zone is to be given top priority. The state council gave the green light for Shanghai to trial China's first free trade zone, the latest step in a national strategy to open up markets and build Shanghai into an international trading and financial hub. The mayor confirmed that the city's customs policies will have to be changed to allow imports to enter and exit the zone without intervention. Institutional innovation is regarded as the key to building the zone, instead of preferential policies. After a series of policies and efforts, Shanghai is continuously moving up global financial center rankings, with a particular good result in the International Financial centers Development Index (2012), placing sixth globally in that ranking.

4.2 The status quo of Shanghai as an IFC

It is clear that Shanghai as an IFC is gaining importance rapidly. The Shanghai Stock Exchange, ultimately the heart of the Shanghai IFC, is already the 7th largest by market capitalization, and growing. Following

APPROACHES AND CHALLENGES

graphic illustrates this:

Tablet 4-1   Largest domestic equity market capitalization at year-end 2012 and 2011

	Exchange	USD bn end-2012	USD bn end-2011	% change in USD	% change in local currency
1	NYSE Euronext (US)	14,086	11,796	19.4%	19.4%
2	NASDAQ OMX (US)	4,582	3,845	19.2%	19.2%
3	Tokyo Stock Exchange Group	3,479	3,325	4.6%	17.6%
4	London Stock Exchange Group	3,397	3,266	4.0%	2.4%
5	NYSE Euronext (Europe)	2,832	2,447	15.8%	14.0%
6	Hong Kong Exchanges	2,832	2,258	25.4%	25.2%
7	Shanghai SE	2,547	2,357	8.1%	7.0%
8	TMX Group	2,059	1,912	7.7%	5.3%
9	Deutsche Börse	1,486	1,185	25.5%	23.6%
10	Australian SE	1,387	1,198	15.7%	14.3

Source: *World Federation of Exchanges, January 2013*

Even though the Shanghai Stock Exchange is at place seven, it is no secret that the potential is far greater. Within years the Shanghai IFC could be regarded as one of the key global IFC's worldwide, and with regards to our secondary research it is apparent that is not a question of if, but when the Shanghai IFC will make a transition from a domestic IFC to a key global IFC.

4.3   Tschoegl's model: identifying current weaknesses of the Shanghai IFC

There are certain factors that are constraining the growth of the

Shanghai IFC that need to be considered by Chinese policy makers, in order to guarantee maximum success. As we systematically identified these factors by using Tschoegl's four dimensional models, we also compared them to Frankfurt, to see how working structures should look like. The following model is the result:

	Shanghai	Frankfurt
Clients	— Not the headquarters of most domestic banks including the major domestic banks — Foreign assets still below 10% in Shanghai	— Headquarters of domestic banks — (need to determine foreign assets percentage)
Geographic Reach	— Promotion not very developed — RMB not convertible — Stock market access to foreigners difficult	— Frankfurt Main Finance used for international promotion — Euro free convertible — Stock market accessible to everyone
Products	— $2.3 trillion market cap (largest in Asia) — Heavily regulated — Lack of high-interest yield financial products — Shadow banking — Needs shipping finance improvement — Heavy need for products such as pension funds	— $1.3 trillion market cap — Over 90% of German stocks traded in Frankfurt — Increasing, medium regulation after financial crisis of 2008 — Domestic banks are universal banks
Value-added Chain	— Recent increase in specialized universities — Lacking qualified employees	— specialized universities — State of the art research and very sizeable talent pool — One of the biggest value-added per employee in Germany

The first dimension: clients

Even though Shanghai is currently the location with most foreign bank subsidiaries it still needs to improve its concentration of both foreign and domestic banks. In 2008, 165 foreign financial institutions were located in Shanghai, which accounts for 24% of all foreign institutions located in China, yet foreign assets on all bank assets only account for under 10% (Boering and Loechel, 2010). Thus, it is not the presence of foreign institutions that is the problem, but the amount of transactions that are happening. This needs to be increased gradually. Ways to encourage this is to continue liberalizing the financial sector through policy. The graphic below shows German banks present in China. This clearly shows that there is already a significant presence.

Secondly, the problem in the clients dimension is the number of domestic bank's headquarters present in Shanghai. Of the 11 banks owned by the central government merely the Bank of Communications has its headquarters in Shanghai (facts and details.com). Other than that the Bank of Shanghai and the Shanghai Pudong Development Bank are the only banks with their headquarters in Shanghai. Admittedly, a truly global IFC must not necessarily have their domestic bank's headquarters in Shanghai, yet it should have sizeable subsidiaries in the IFC, which is still at a sub-par level in Shanghai, since only 176,000 jobs are available in the financial services industry as of 2007. Shanghai as second biggest port in the world would also benefit from more bank know-how in Shanghai, as shipping finance is key (Boering and Loechel, 2010).

What can be learned from Frankfurt?

Frankfurt is one of the biggest cities in Germany, and while it can in no way be to Shanghai in population size, 37% of its total employment works in the financial services sector (Boering and Loechel, 2010), whereas in Shanghai it is a mere 3.4%. Since Shanghai's population is far greater, it may be unrealistic to aim for a figure close to 37%, but it shall also be said that Shanghai is aiming to become an international financial center with far greater magnitude than Frankfurt. In its nature, Shanghai's financial sector will thus have to be significantly bigger. In London for example, 300,000 individuals are currently working in the financial services sector, which amounts to nearly twice as many individuals as Shanghai (Boering and Loechel, 2010). Hence, looking at these numbers, it is clear that Shanghai as an IFC needs to create more jobs in this industry. However, this is something that may automatically happen when other measures are taken to expand the IFC Shanghai, yet it is certainly something to think more about.

The second dimension: geographic reach
At present Shanghai's promotional mix on behalf of the financial services office is still lacking reach and "buzz". This means that Shanghai's international brand should be pushed in a greater fashion, in order to attract more attention. Secondly, the lack of a freely convertible currency discourages more financial activity in Shanghai. China needs to allow for further exchange rate flexibility, as well as allow a greater amount of offshore Renminbi deposits in the PRC.

In order to compensate this perceived risk of foreign investors, developing larger and deeper financial markets is vitally important. Bond markets and derivative markets need to be expanded, in order for foreign investors to be able to hedge against currency and other risk. Products such as currency swaps need to be encouraged in order to further increase business activity. China has already promoted international trade contracts such as swap lines, in order to supply foreign central banks with Renminbi, which has increased the use of Renminbi in China's trade from 3 to 10 percent in 2012. Yet, the Renminbi is only the 17th currency worldwide in respect of the total value of cross-border transactions, representing 0.5% of the value of all transactions through SWIFT (OECD Economic Surveys China, 2013). This will undoubtedly change in the near future though as China engages in further policy to encourage Renminbi trade. An HSBC survey suggests that this figure will be around one-third of China's trade. If China wants Renminbi to become an international currency, competing with the US dollar and the Euro, it needs to liberalize the Renminbi as much as possible. Doing this would greatly increase Shanghai IFC's role in the financial world of today. Not only is the Renminbi regulated fiercely but the stock market needs to be accessible to more potential investors. At the moment, a very limited number of foreign investors are permitted to invest in the Shanghai Stock Exchange. The so called qualified foreign institutional investors (QFII) that are permitted to invest have risen from 33 in 2005 to 207 in 2012 (McKinsey Quarterly 3, 2013), yet this is by no means enough for Shanghai to transition from a domestic IFC to a global one.

What can be learned from Frankfurt?

Looking at the promotional aspect, Shanghai should consider Frankfurt's approach. Frankfurt has created the Frankfurt Main Finance office, which is its marketing institution. Its website Frankfurt-main-finance.com is set up extremely well and is full of useful information for any stakeholder interested in Frankfurt as an IFC. Furthermore, it uses social media and other innovative channels to reach its target audience, constantly offering information and service. This is an approach that Shanghai could approach, in order to attract more attention and create a certain "buzz" around their financial center.

The Third Dimension: Products

China's financial sector is still one of the most regulated in the world. This needs to be further liberalized, in order for more investment activity to occur. As stated above, bond markets and derivatives markets, and currency swap lines need to be further established in order to compensate for the lack of a free floating and convertible currency. Furthermore, it is possible at the moment to trade convertibles, derivatives, commodity-futures, options, exchange-traded-funds, repos, company and treasury bonds are available for trading (Boering and Loechel, 2010). Yet, in the present financial world these products are only a small fraction of the financial instruments available. If Shanghai wishes to become a global IFC, it needs to offer state of the art, innovative financial products. As mentioned before, ICT does threaten some of an IFC's activity, as computerized trading has become very popular, yet if the Shanghai IFC encourages high-end tertiary financial services, such as, but not exclusively, venture capital and hedge fund firms it may be able to create a much needed competitive advantage over other IFC's. It is by no means to say that China has not made an effort to innovate this sector, as the bond market for example has risen to become the world's third largest in recent years, and the short-term commercial paper market has also recently greatly increased. (OECD Economic Surveys China, 2013). Yet, with regard to China's economic potential, the activity of financial instruments is still to be considered rather low.

The lack of high-yield and high interest financial instruments has caused problems in the Chinese economy. Shadow banking is a term which refers to the creation of credit across the financial system, which is not subject to regular oversight (Investopedia). When done in large quantities shadow banking creates many problems, such as losing monetary control over the nation. Hikes in private interest rates reduce the incentives for individuals to take out money from the bank, and the incentive for shadow banking, in the form of credit creation increases. This is the exact phenomenon that has happened recently, as the People's Bank of China has reported an increase in RMB deposits of 9.6 trillion yuan in 2011. In addition, loan volume decreased by 2.3 trillion yuan in the same period (Deloitte China, 2012). The supervisory and regulatory authority has recognized this problem and has created regulations to make it better. However, it seems that this problem will not be fixed by mere policy measures. Artificial interest rates seem to be a major reason for this phenomenon, as interest rate manipulation has negatively impacted market-based reforms. In the short term further policy and regulation may be necessary to stop this problem from getting out of hand, however in the long run further movement to market-determined interest rates is needed. When market-determined interest rates take over, there will be fewer incentives for shadow banking. In addition, as an IFC profits from all institutional activity, a decrease in shadow banking and an increase in institutional lending will have great benefits for Shanghai as an IFC.

Another negative effect of the lack of investment opportunities is the heavy rise of real estate prices. With low interest rate financial products the incentives to invest in real estate becomes significantly higher. Some may call this phenomenon a housing bubble, yet even if it is to be considered one, there are a number of factors that are likely to keep the Chinese economy from suffering major setbacks. First of all, the down payment on property is 30% for first time homeowners, and 50% for buyers of second homes (Hennessy, 2012). This is to discourage investors making quick profits, by speculating on property prices. Secondly, derivatives such as credit default swaps (CDS) are illegal in China, making it significantly less appealing for large-scale investors to invest in the real estate market. Lastly, and most importantly China's rapid urbanization is in dire need of new real estate, as Stephen Roach, a Yale professor states … But the pessimists' hype overlooks one of the most important drivers of China's modernization: the greatest urbanization story the world has ever seen. In 2011, the urban share of the Chinese population surpassed 50% for the first time, reaching 51.3%, compared to less than 20% in 1980 … China cannot afford to wait to build its new cities. Instead, investment and construction must be aligned with the future influx of urban dwellers. The "ghost city" critique misses this point entirely…" Hence, it is by no means to say that a housing bubble will create severe problems for the Chinese economy, however this trend does show the lack of financial instruments investors can put their money in, and with an increase of investment options, fewer investors will revert to real estate investment.

The lack of financial products clearly restricts individuals in their financial planning, and with regards to the aging population of China one financial product would greatly benefit China in particular, pension funds. Highly innovative pension fund systems could be devised, that could help alleviate the future economic pressure China will be under due to this phenomenon.

China's elderly population is projected to continue increasing rapidly.

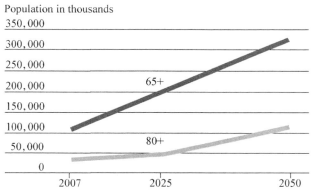

Source: United Nations, *World Population Ageing 2007* (New York: UN Dept. of Economic and Social Affairs, Population Division, 2007): 202-203.

The table above shows the great increase in the elderly population in China, and thus it is clear that a pension fund would find demand. It is issues such as these, where creating innovative financial instruments that aid those needs can create competitive advantages for IFC's. Creating an innovative pension fund could lead to other nations facing similar problems adopting this approach. As Europe and many other regions in the world are currently witnessing an aging population, it is easily conceivable that a product like this would spark some interest from abroad.

What can be learned from Frankfurt?

Frankfurt as an IFC has gained in importance after the financial crisis 2008, which was not necessarily to be expected. Recently, through EU government policy, financial regulation has taken place, yet not to an extent where it could have severe harm on the financial services industry. As China's and Europe's political systems are inherently different, the low degree of financial regulation that exists in Europe may not be successfully implementable in China. However, Frankfurt stands as a good example that relatively low regulation in the financial sector can work, and deregulation must not in nature be looked as bad. Hence, taking the Frankfurt case under consideration, China could potentially increase its rate of deregulation of the financial services sector, in order to speed up the growth of the Shanghai IFC.

The fourth dimension: value-added chain

It is clear that a new established IFC needs to guarantee education and know-how at the highest level. Looking at education, Shanghai is already offering excellent finance programs, from a handful of institutions such as the Shanghai Finance University, Fudan University, CEIBS, and the Jiao Tong University. International exchange programs are encouraged here, in order to, like in any subject create educational synergy effects, and exchange know-how. When it comes to the status quo and finance professionals, it may be important to recruit internationally. Individuals who have over a decade of experience in other markets like London, New York or Frankfurt, could be of vital importance, in order to gain know-how from already existing global IFC's (Boering and Loechel, 2010)

Germany is a country known for its excellent vocational training opportunities. This is an approach that could be adopted in Shanghai. Certain jobs in the finance industry are extremely specialized, and whilst they are quite complex, they do not require a broad skill set. In these cases, it can be of benefit to give these employees specific training in their field, instead of sending them to get a general Finance degree at a University.

4.4 The big picture

Looking at all the aspects from Tschoegl's model that were discussed, it is clear that China is moving in the right direction, by structurally liberalizing the financial sector, yet it is also clear that further action is needed. In the client's dimension, Shanghai needs to be given more focus in the financial scope of China. Most headquarters of big banks are located in Beijing, and whilst this does not necessarily need to change, there does need to be an increase in strategic subsidiary units located in Shanghai. Currently the number of financial services jobs in Shanghai is far too low to compete with global financial centers around the world.

Foreign firms need to be further encouraged to enter Shanghai, domestic banks should be urged to expand their business activity in Shanghai, and general liberalization of the financial sector will also help increase financial services jobs. Deregulating the financial sector specifically means deregulating the Renminbi through techniques described above, allowing more foreign investors to invest in the Shanghai Stock Exchange, and allowing more financial products to be traded. Furthermore, interest rates should increasingly be determined by market-forces, rather than artificially. At present there is simply a lack of high yield, high interest financial instruments, which has caused both shadow banking and real estate speculation to increase. As stated above, even if these phenomena are exaggerated by foreign media, finding solutions for these would greatly benefit the financial sector. It is through innovative and sustainable financial instruments, that Shanghai can establish itself as a global financial center. One innovative product suggested above, would be a pension fund that would alleviate the pressure an aging population brings along. Not only would this solve problems domestically, but also this solution could be exported worldwide, as the aging population conflict does not only exist in China.

5 Conclusions

In conclusion, it is no secret that within the next decade Shanghai will become one of the most important financial centers worldwide. With approximately 3.5 trillion US dollars in currency reserves today and steady economic growth, China has equipped itself with ideal preconditions to develop into an ever bigger economic superpower. As China is transitioning away from being an export nation that relies heavily on low labor costs, it is moving towards an economy dominated by the tertiary sector. Thus, it is vitally important for Shanghai to develop into a key global financial center, and it is on its way to do so. The Shanghai Stock Exchange has already reached a market capitalization of 2,547 billion USD in 2012, which makes it the 7th largest stock exchange worldwide.

In order to further facilitate the transition from a domestic to a global financial center, several aspects need to be considered. Shanghai needs to be given the absolute financial focus within China, having big domestic bank subsidiaries, as well as a high number of foreign institutions that are not only present but also increase the relatively low amount of foreign assets that presently exist. In addition, financial deregulation of the Renminbi, the Shanghai Stock Exchange, and financial instruments is key. There needs to be an increase in investment opportunities, in order to discourage economic problems such as shadow banking and a housing bubble. Hence, moving away from artificially set interest rates and towards more market-determined interest rates is important. As the case study of Frankfurt shows, it will also be important to consider the development of ICT, and to focus on high-end and highly complex financial services in an innovative manner, as these jobs are less likely to become threatened by computer trading and other technological advancements.

The Chinese Government is clearly continuously deregulating the financial sector in order to further improve the financial climate in China. The central government has undoubtedly realized the importance of an IFC in Shanghai, as proves what Han Zheng mentioned on May 31st. He stated that finance is the core of the modern economy, and that great priority was going to be given to financial innovation, including such things as Renminbi innovation. With this in mind, it is almost certain that Shanghai will successfully develop into one of the major global financial players within the next decade, as the factors we determined to be of importance in our research are dealt with in an effective manner.

References

2012 China Banking Industry. (2013). Top Ten Trends and Outlook. Deloitte China. N.p., n.d. Web. 01.

Best Conditions for Your Success. (2013). Frankfurt Main Finance E.V.: Why Frankfurt. N.p., n.d. Web. 01.

Boeing, P. S., and Loechel, H. (2010). *The Present State of Shanghai as an International Financial center: A Comparison with London and Frankfurt*. EU-China Business Management Training Working Paper No. 11. Available at SSRN: http: //ssrn.com/abstract=1714402.

European Central Bank. (2012). Financial Integration in Europe.

Grote, M. H. (2008). Foreign banks' attraction to the financial center Frankfurt—an inverted "U"-shaped relationship. *Journal of Economic Geography*, 8(2), 239-258.

Handke, W. (1988). Finanzplatz Shanghai. *Zeitschrift für das gesamte Kreditwesen*, (41)1, 1.

Hennessy, M. P. (2012). *China: A real estate bubble, or no trouble?* Morgan Creek Capital Management.

Kindleberger, C. P. (1973). *The formation of financial centers: A study in comparative economic history*. Available at http: //hdl.handle.net/1721.1/63624.

OECD (2013). *OECD Economic Surveys: China 2013*, OECD Publishing. doi: 10.1787/eco_surveys-chn-2013-en.

Olds, K. (1997). Globalizing Shanghai: the "global intelligence corps" and the building of Pudong, *Cities*, (14)2, 109-123.

The Mckinsey Quarterly 3. (2013). New York: McKinsey & Co.

Tschoegl, A. (2000). International Banking centers, Geography and Foreign Banks, in: Financial markets, institutions & instruments, (9)1, 1-34.

WFE Publishes. (2012). Global Market Highlights, World Federation of Exchanges. WFE Publishes 2012 Global Market Highlights, World Federation of Exchanges. N.p., n.d. Web. 02 Aug. 2013.

World Urbanization Prospects, the 2011 Revision. (2013). N.p., n.d. Web. 02.

Wu, F. L. (2003). Globalization, place promotion and urban development in Shanghai. *Journal of Urban Affairs*, (25)1, 55-78.

Wu, F. L. (2000). Place promotion in Shanghai, PRC. *Cities*, (17)5, 349-361.

Zhao, SXB., Zhang, L., and Wang, D. T. (2004). Determining factors of the development of a national financial center: the case of China. *Geoforun*, (35)5, 577-592.

Appendix 1 (Boering and Loechel)

	London	Frankfurt	Shanghai
Clients	— Bank of England located in London — Capital of UK — Headquarters of domestic banks — Number one position for international banks European headquarters — Branches and subsidiaries of foreign banks: 250 (in 2008); — 50% of European investment banking activity is concentrated in London — Higher number of foreign listed companies than any other stock exchange in the world — Employees in financial services: 300,000 in Greater London (in 2007), 43% of total employment — International port city — *Evaluation: high*	— Bundesbank located in Frankfurt — European Central Bank located in Frankfurt — Frankfurt is not the capital — Headquarters of domestic banks — Branches and subsidiaries of foreign banks: 140 (in 2008) — Regulators (European/ domestic) partly located in Frankfurt — Employees in financial services: 75,000 in Frankfurt (in 2007), 37% of total employment — No port city — *Evaluation: medium/high*	— People's Bank of China not located in Shanghai, only a sub-branch — Shanghai is not the capital — Regulators not located in Shangahai, only sub-branches — No (or just very few) headquarters of domestic banks — Branches and subsidiaries of foreign banks: 165 (in 2008), 24% of all 689 financial institutions, share of foreign assets on all bank assets under 10% — Highest concentration of foreign financial institutions in China — Employees in financial services: 176,000 in Shanghai (in 2007), 3.4% of total employment — International port city, 2nd largest port in the world — *Evaluation: medium*

APPROACHES AND CHALLENGES

continued

	London	Frankfurt	Shanghai
Geographic Reach	— Global financial centre — Global gateway to Europe — Characteristics of an off-shore centre — Mobility is high: incl. airports, traffic and hotels — Communication infrastructure is well developed — Loosing business to other niche-centres — International promotion activities are fragmented — *Evaluation: high*	— Interregional financial centre, with strong linkages to other European financial centres — Characteristics of an on-shore centre — Mobility is high: incl. airports, traffic and hotels — Communication infrastructure is well developed — International promotion activities are concerted via *Frankfurt Main Finance;* — *Evaluation: medium*	— Domestic financial centre — Characteristic of an on-shore centre — Financial markets still relatively isolated, non-convertibility of RMB — Mobility is medium-high: incl,. airports, traffic and hotels — Communication infrastructure is fair-medium developed — International promotion still in initial phase — Involved agencies and institutions are highly decentralized — *Evaluation: low*

Appendix 2 (Boering and Loechel)

Products	— Low level of regulation, but challenged by increasing pan-European regulation — Strong position of stock markets	— Medium level of regulation, supported by increasing pan-European regulation — German Stock Exchange:	— High level of regulation, but challenged by increasingly streamlined international regulations — Weak position of

continued

| Products | — Derivative Trading: biggest market in the world
— FX market: biggest in the world (35% of global turnover)
— Reinsurance market biggest in the world
— International insurance market, biggest in the world (gross premium income of 40 bn. USD in 2007)
— Foreign equity trading: a leading centre
— International IPOs: a leading centre
— Separated and specialised banks | turnover of 1.6 bn. USD, number 7 in the world
— 90% of German stocks traded in Frankfurt
— Low internationalisation of primary markets (2001-2008: only 7 foreign IPOs vs. 148 domestic ones: 4.8% of IPOs foreign dimension
— Domestic banks are universal banks
— High level of outstanding commercial bank loans
— Re-regionalization of foreign banks in Germany, moving away from financial centres, number of finance related jobs is decreasing | segmented stock markets, external financing via bonds and stocks only 10.1 and 3.9% in 2006)
— Bond market dominated by treasury and PBOC bonds, 70% of all company bonds issued by state-owned companies
— Main share of tradable shares in hold by individual investors, result is immense volatility in the market
— Products available: convertibles, derivatives, commodity-futures, options, ETFs, repos, company and treasure bonds
— Gold Exchange: world largest gold spot market in 2008
— Future Exchange: copper, |

continued

Products			— aluminum, zinc, steel wire rod, rebar, natural rubber, fuel oil and gold — Market capitalization in June 2009: 2,330 bn. USD, 2nd largest in Asia in 2008 — Domestic banks are specialised banks — Strong position of banking sector, external financing via commercial loans 84.9% in 2006
	— *Evaluation: high*	— *Evaluation: medium*	— *Evaluation: low/ medium*
Value-added Chain	— Value-added per employee is 50% above UK average — Big talent pool and level of research — High number of top universities (14% students coming from abroad) — *Evaluation: high*	— Value-added per employee is 50% above Germany's average — Big talent pool and level of research — Number of specialised universities — *Evaluation: high*	— Value-added per employee is not known — Too small talent pool and level of research — A Number of specialised universities — *Evaluation: low/ medium*

图书在版编目(CIP)数据

路径与挑战:不同视角下的上海国际金融中心建设 = Approaches and Challenges: Different Perspectives for Building Shanghai Financial Center:英文/贺瑛,张树义主编. —上海:复旦大学出版社,2014.12
ISBN 978-7-309-10520-9

Ⅰ.路… Ⅱ.①贺…②张… Ⅲ.国际金融中心-上海市-文集-英文 Ⅳ.F832.751

中国版本图书馆 CIP 数据核字(2014)第 064541 号

路径与挑战:不同视角下的上海国际金融中心建设
贺 瑛 张树义 主编
责任编辑/王联合 张咏梅

复旦大学出版社有限公司出版发行
上海市国权路 579 号 邮编:200433
网址:fupnet@fudanpress.com http://www.fudanpress.com
门市零售:86-21-65642857 团体订购:86-21-65118853
外埠邮购:86-21-65109143
江苏凤凰数码印务有限公司

开本 890×1240 1/32 印张 5 字数 145 千
2014 年 12 月第 1 版第 1 次印刷

ISBN 978-7-309-10520-9/F·2027
定价:25.00 元

如有印装质量问题,请向复旦大学出版社有限公司发行部调换。
版权所有 侵权必究